Religion in America

ADVISORY EDITOR

Edwin S. Gaustad

THE SALVATION ARMY IN AMERICA

Selected Reports, 1899-1903

Frederick Booth-Tucker

ARNO PRESS
A NEW YORK TIMES COMPANY
New York • 1972

Reprint Edition 1972 by Arno Press Inc.

Farm Colonies of the Salvation Army was reprinted
from a copy in The Wesleyan University Library

RELIGION IN AMERICA - Series II
ISBN for complete set: 0-405-04050-4
See last pages of this volume for titles.

Manufactured in the United States of America

Library of Congress Cataloging in Publication Data

Booth Tucker, Frederick St. George de Lautour,
    1853-1929.
    The Salvation Army in America.

    (Religion in America, series II)
    CONTENTS: Farm colonies of the Salvation Army
[first published in 1903]--The Salvation Army in the
United States [first published in 1899]--The social
relief work of the Salvation Army in the United States
[first published in 1900] [etc.]
    1. Salvation Army--U. S. I. Title.
BX9716.B68 1972   267'.15'0973   79-38439
ISBN 0-405-04060-1

Contents

Booth-Tucker, Frederick

Farm Colonies of the Salvation Army. (*Reprinted from* **Bulletin of the Bureau of Labor,** No. 48, Sept., 1903.) Washington, D. C., 1903.

The Salvation Army in the United States. New York, 1899.

The Social Relief Work of the Salvation Army in the United States. (*Reprinted from* **Monographs on American Social Economics,** Vol. XX. Edited by Herbert B. Adams. 1900.)

The Salvation Army as a Temperance Movement. New York, n.d.

FARM COLONIES OF THE SALVATION ARMY

Commander Booth Tucker

1903

BULLETIN

BUREAU OF LABOR.

No. 48. WASHINGTON. SEPTEMBER, 1903.

EDITORIAL NOTE.

By act of Congress of February 14, 1903, the Department of Commerce and Labor was established and the existing Department of Labor was placed under its jurisdiction and made one of its bureaus. The title of this office has, therefore, by direction of the Secretary of Commerce and Labor, been changed to the Bureau of Labor, and future Bulletins and reports will bear that name, but will be numbered in continuation of the series of the former Department of Labor.

C. D. W.

FARM COLONIES OF THE SALVATION ARMY.

BY COMMANDER BOOTH TUCKER.

The farm colonies of the Salvation Army in the United States were first organized in the spring of 1898 for the purpose of enabling stranded but worthy families to keep together and ultimately, by their own exertions and payments, to become home owners. Experience has shown that, while it is comparatively easy to take care of the unmarried poor in the cities, and to find sufficiently remunerative work for them there, the case is different with the family.

In case of sickness or loss of work the position of the women and children is especially distressing. Rent has to be paid, hungry mouths have to be fed, clothing must be provided, and the numerous requirements of a growing family must be met.

It is stated that in London 3,000 families consisting of 9 persons each, 7,000 of 8, and 23,000 of 6 or 7, live huddled together in dwellings of but one room. The furniture ordinarily consists of one bed, and as many as can do so get into it, while the others sleep under it, that being the next warmest place.

While conditions are not at present so bad in American cities, they are rapidly trending in the same direction. Hence the colonies of the

Salvation Army were specially organized for the purpose of relieving city congestion and of preventing families from being broken up, the theory of redemption being thus formulated: "Place the waste labor on the waste land by means of the waste capital and thereby convert the trinity of waste into a unity of production;" or, as it has been tersely put by one of our great writers and thinkers, "The landless man to the manless land."

In the United States the experiment now comprises the following three colonies: (1) Fort Amity, in Colorado, in the fertile valley of the River Arkansas; (2) Fort Romie, in California, not far from the famous Hotel del Monte, near the Bay of Monterey; (3) Fort Herrick, in Ohio, about 20 miles from the city of Cleveland.

FORT AMITY, COLO.

Early in April, 1898, a section of land consisting of 640 acres (since increased to nearly 2,000) was purchased in the neighborhood of Holly, on the line of the Atchison, Topeka and Santa Fe Railroad, 267 miles east of Denver, in the valley of the Arkansas River. An abundant supply of water from the Buffalo Canal is supplemented by a still more abundant subsurface underflow, while an immense system of inland reservoirs in course of construction will serve to irrigate a vast tract of land in the neighborhood. Hence this colony has an almost unlimited opportunity for expansion and is the most important under control of the Salvation Army. The soil is rich and the climate superb, the elevation being some 3,500 feet above the level of the sea, thus avoiding the extremes of heat and cold. The mining camps of Colorado afford an excellent market on the one hand, while on the other the colony is on the highway to the principal cattle markets of the midwestern States, being linked to both by the Santa Fe Railroad.

The principal crops include the famous "netted gem" cantaloupe, for which Colorado has gained a great reputation. The recent establishment of a beet-sugar factory in the valley of the Arkansas River, within easy reach of the colony, has brought to its very doors a market for another valuable crop for which good prices can be obtained.

For stock raising the valley is probably without its equal, being on the way to the Kansas City and Chicago stock yards. Here the alfalfa, or lucerne, on which cattle and hogs so quickly fatten, flourishes in rich profusion, requiring but little care beyond occasional watering and being cut several times year after year without replanting. Alfalfa also produces the best quality of butter and honey, for both of which products the valley is famous. At the same time the boundless prairies which surround the colony furnish pasture for the greater part of the year. For berries, fruit, cabbages, onions, and other agricultural produce the soil is also admirably suited.

It is intended in the near future to establish an extensive sanitarium for working men. The need for such an institution has been keenly felt for many years. It would, moreover, provide a home market for the colonist's produce. An orphanage has been erected, at a cost of $20,000, with the intention that as orphans grow up they may marry and settle upon the land, forming ultimately the best colonists.

An agricultural credit association has recently been established, modeled upon the plan of the Raiffeisen village loan associations of Germany. This is believed to be the first experiment of the kind in America, although the system has been highly recommended by the United States Government.[a]

Two schoolhouses have been established in the colony by the county and will shortly be replaced by a much larger building. Their capacity is already taxed to the utmost, the children of school age numbering 140. A post and money order office has also been established. The recent erection by the railroad company of a freight depot with siding has further enhanced the value of the colony and improved its prospects. Plans have lately been made for a passenger depot, the building of which will be begun at once.

There are now about 300 colonists, including men, women, and children, in the Fort Amity colony.

FORT ROMIE, CAL.

Nestled in the beautiful valley of the Salinas River, near the bay of Monterey, is the California colony. A fine sweep of 519 acres of rich agricultural land has been purchased. The land has been divided into 10-acre tracts, cottages have been built, and an irrigation pumping plant has been erected to supply water from the river.

The soil is admirably adapted to the growth of potatoes, sugar beets, and alfalfa, as well as almost every other variety of agricultural produce. The nearness of the famous beet-sugar factories of Mr. Claus Spreckels at Watsonville and at Salinas renders the success of this colony doubly certain. The valley is famed for its potatoes, which command the highest market price.

There are now about 70 colonists, including men, women, and children, in this colony. One family has already paid for its holding.

FORT HERRICK, OHIO.

Within about 20 miles of the city of Cleveland and close to the childhood home of President Garfield, at Mentor, is a beautiful sweep of level land, fringed with a second growth of wood on its western boundary and containing about 288 acres. The entire tract has been cultivated, several cottages erected, and 33 persons settled.

---

a Cooperative Credit Associations in certain European Countries. Report No. 3, Miscellaneous Series, Division of Statistics, United States Department of Agriculture, 1892.

The owners of the land, Hon. Myron T. Herrick and Mr. James Parmelee, have deeded the land to the Salvation Army for colonization purposes, and the citizens of Cleveland, together with some other friends, have contributed $20,000 toward the enterprise. This extremely generous action will give a splendid start to the Ohio colony, and the intention is to make it a model institution of the kind and an important training ground for the colonies in the West. A small schoolhouse has been built, drinking water is being piped from springs in the neighborhood, and part of the land is about to be tile drained.

COLONY FINANCE.

As the colonies are intended for the worthy families of the city poor, who often have no money even for their traveling expenses, it becomes necessary to provide the capital. The fact that the surplus population of the great cities does not more readily transfer itself to the country districts is not due, as is often supposed, to their attachment to the former and dislike for the latter. If the necessary capital is forthcoming, and they are placed in a position to become home owners, and not mere tenants or farm laborers, the movement of population can be carried out with celerity and success.

Another mistake commonly made in the attempted removal of the city poor has been the effort to colonize the unmarried poor. This is false economy. The family will prove cheaper in the long run, since the wife and children supply unpaid labor. To illustrate: On one of the colonies at the time of a recent visit the father was found cultivating his own land, while the children were earning as much as $2 daily, picking berries for a neighboring farmer. The wife meanwhile looked after the house, the baby, the meals, and the poultry. All were busy, all were earning money. The family had but recently arrived, and were already self-supporting. It was only necessary to find them a cottage, team, agricultural implements, and seed.

In another case the father was able to make good wages as a carpenter, putting up cottages and barns for the colony and neighbors, while the wife and children looked after the home and farm. Five acres were sufficient to supplement his earnings.

Hence it is seen that with management and the selection of a tract of good land, the main requirement is a sufficiency of capital to erect cottages, purchase live stock and implements, and meet traveling and other expenses. The average cost per family amounts to $500, apart from payments for land, and exclusive of general land improvements, such as irrigation works, water supply, and other general utilities. For this sum a family can be fairly launched.

For the purpose of raising the necessary funds, thirty-year gold bonds for $150,000 have been issued on the Colorado and California colonies. Interest is payable semiannually at 5 per cent. A sinking fund of 2 per cent has been established, and the bonds are guaranteed by the Salvation Army, Incorporated.

In addition to the above a colony endowment fund, consisting of donations, has been organized. This fund now amounts to about $30,000. The money is loaned to the colonists in the usual way, being reinvested as fast as it is repaid.

The colonists receive a contract for the purchase of the land and cottage, and are supplied with live stock and implements, a regular account being furnished to the head of each family at stated intervals, showing his indebtedness. The sense of ownership is from the first cultivated, with excellent results. The experience of the Salvation Army is adverse to community of ownership in such settlements. Such ownership usually results in the lazy doing nothing and expecting everything, while the industrious do everything and get nothing—at least nothing commensurate with their toil. Thus a premium is placed upon idleness. This commonly ends in the industrious becoming discouraged, pulling out, and going where they can get the rewards of their industry. The others are then quickly scattered.

The first colonists reached Fort Amity in April, 1898. Most of them had their own household goods. Here and there one had a team of his own. Otherwise they were simply workingmen from the large cities, chiefly New York, who had been unable to accumulate any property. Their railroad fares were paid and their goods shipped to Fort Amity. They were settled upon plots of from 10 to 20 acres each, received a house to live in, the necessary tools and implements, a horse or two each, one or two cows, pigs, and poultry.

The cost of all this was a debt against the colonist. The first were set to work making improvements—irrigating ditches, fences, etc. They were allowed the current rate of wages, $2 a day. Half of this was credited on their debt, the other dollar paid their living expenses until the returns from their land began to come in. In April, 1902, the first colonist discharged his entire debt to the Army. He arrived at Fort Amity in March, 1899, his entire capital, the savings of ten or twelve years of married life, being a team and some household furniture. He has now 20 acres with a neat stone cottage built by himself, all free from incumbrance. His entire debt to the Army was $900. In three years he paid it off, besides supporting a wife and three children and building his house.

The rapid increase in land values caused by the close settlement of the land serves to protect the investment from any probability of loss. For instance, unimproved land which was bought for from $20 to $27 an acre is now selling at $40, while the colonists value the same land improved at $100, and sales have been made at even a higher price. In another colony land which was bought for $50 is selling for $100.

As an explanation of the comparatively high prices of the land it should be explained that it has been deemed wise to pay the best prices for good soil, it being regarded as false economy to get poor land even as a gift, since the expenditure and improvements cost the same in either case, while the return is far greater if the soil is good.

The question is frequently asked whether any difficulty is found in recovering payments from the colonists. To this the following reply may be made:

1. So far from the colonists being unwilling to meet their liabilities they are eager to pay them off at the earliest possible moment.

2. Even were this not the case the rapid rise in land values would afford sufficient protection from loss.

3. An experience of nearly five years has shown that few outlets for capital are known so absolutely free from risk as colonization schemes of this kind, provided, of course, the enterprise be honestly and sensibly managed. It must be remembered that this statement is made after an experience with two severe droughts, insect pests, heavy interest for borrowed capital, repayments of short loans, insufficiency of capital, and serious variations of market in the sale of the produce, so that it can not be said that the success of the experiment has been due to an absence of the ordinary difficulties with which agricultural operations must necessarily contend.

In this connection the words of Mr. James A. Davis, the industrial commissioner of the Santa Fe Railroad, who has watched the colony in Colorado from its inception and is familiar with all its workings, may be quoted: "As a colonization plan it is the most practical and feasible that has ever come to my attention. As an investment I consider it sound." To these words may be added the following letter from the late President Benjamin Harrison:

I recall with pleasure my conversation with you in which you outlined your plans for colonizing the poor of our great cities on small homestead farms. I was much interested in what you said, as the work seemed to have great promise in it, especially in view of what seemed to me the very practical and business-like lines on which you had laid it down. It is a very pitiful thing to see industrious and worthy people who have been enticed from their country homes into the city, and are bound there hand and foot by their inability to accumulate enough to get back to the life in which they were reared, and in which they might have success. Your plan to make a thorough inquiry into the adaptation of the people to be helped, and not to take any except those whose habits seem to promise success, and to help these, not by gifts that pauperize, but by loans to be repaid, seems to me to be highly wise and commendable.

FARM COLONIES IN SOUTH AFRICA.

Several farm colonies have been established by the Salvation Army in South Africa. On a small farm near Cape Colony needy whites are taken care of when stranded, and are provided with a temporary home and work. The Government allows an annual grant of $1,000 toward the expenses.

A tract of 3,000 acres has been granted to the Salvation Army in Rhodesia and two similar tracts in Zululand for the formation of native settlements. The work has made considerable progress in spite of the war, the labors of the Salvation Army officers receiving the warmest encouragement, both from Boers and from British officials.

FARM COLONIES IN AUSTRALIA.

A large tract of valuable land, covering 20,000 acres, has recently been deeded to the Salvation Army in Western Australia by the Government for colonization purposes. As a rule no individual grant is allowed to exceed 5,000 acres, but in the present instance a special exception was made by the legislature, for the purpose of assisting in the efforts to settle the worthy poor.

The Collie settlement is situated in the southwestern portion of Western Australia, 125 miles by rail from Perth and 40 miles by rail from the nearest seaport town, Bunbury. The celebrated coal mines of the Collie River are 3 miles from the settlement. The 20,000 acres consist of forest, scrub, and open country, with 17 miles of river frontage. A large number of paddocks have been fenced and the outer boundaries are nearing completion. The various colony buildings are now being erected and will include a large home for boys at Gibb's Ford and a girls' home at Pollard's Homestead.

In addition to the above tract of land, several smaller colonies have been established, occupying nearly 3,000 acres, and including three industrial farms for criminal and neglected boys, and three industrial homes for girls, with total accommodations for 362. There is also a home for aged men. Toward the above homes and farms the Australian Government contributes annual grants amounting to $15,000, the total annual expenditure of the Salvation Army upon them amounting (exclusive of Collie) to $45,000.

SALVATION ARMY LAND AND INDUSTRIAL COLONY AT HADLEIGH, NEAR LONDON, ESSEX, ENGLAND.[a]

This colony is situated near the mouth of the Thames, about 30 miles from London. Many sites were offered, but the one at Hadleigh comprising about 3,000 acres was selected as being the most likely to afford the greatest number of advantages, because of its geographical situation. The colony comprises a tract of land extending from the vicinity of Benfleet Station to Leigh Station, on the London, Tilbury and Southend Railway—a distance of 3 miles.

[a] The information relating to the Hadleigh colony was furnished by Colonel Lamb, the manager of the colony.

This railway flanks the southern side of the settlement and cuts through the southeast portion. Beyond is the fore shore of the Essex coast. The London main road to Southend passes through the northern side.

The colony has been divided into sections, as follows, each under a responsible superintendent:

	Acres.
Arable farm land	600
Pasture land	1,000
Market garden	300
Brick field, No. 1 ⎫	
Brick field, No. 2 ⎬ about	100
Brick field, No. 3 ⎭	
Fore shore and fishing	1,000
Total	3,000

The expenditures for the Hadleigh colony have been approximately as follows:

Original cost of the land	$200,000
Buildings, railways, wharf, and other necessities	125,000
Purchase of adjoining lands	125,000
Cattle, sheep, horses, and general stock	100,000
Wagons, machinery, implements, etc	50,000
Total	600,000

The gates of the colony are open to every destitute man, irrespective of creed or nationality. The bulk of the men are housed in dormitories, classified according to the character of the men and other conditions generally.

Admission dormitory contains about 30 beds. As the individual progresses in usefulness and good conduct, he is promoted step by step until he reaches the dormitory, constructed internally to accommodate only 3 men in one room.

A grade above this is Castle House, with sleeping accommodation for some 30 men. This is chiefly reserved for timekeepers, foremen, and others of good character.

The highest class is Park House, a select residence situated in the center of the market garden, which can accommodate only about 20. The essential qualification for admission to this enviable retreat is an irreproachable character. The object of thus grading the men is to hold before them a constant inducement for self-improvement. The motto of each grade is "excelsior."

LABOR CONDITIONS.

The labor of the colony, instead of being cheaper, is on the whole more expensive than that of other employers, because of the excessive amount it costs to maintain a large section of almost useless workers. Owing to the character of the colony there is always a large proportion

of "wastrels" continually on hand, whose labor, during the probationary period of six weeks or three months, can not by any means be
reckoned as an equivalent for their maintenance. The ordinary
employer rejects this class entirely and, moreover, in slack seasons dis-
penses with a number of his average hands, whose rate of wages here
is equal to that obtainable outside.

There is also a considerable number of those who are permanently
incapable, either from old age or other causes. These constitute a
serious incumbrance, from a commercial standpoint, which the ordi-
nary•employer has not to reckon with. This drawback, however, is
counterbalanced to a considerable extent in the case of workhouse
men by the subsidies of the boards of guardians, and is likely to be
more so by the Government subsidies which the colony is likely to
receive in the near future.

The administration of the colony is, however, for this and other reasons, more expensive than that of an ordinary commercial undertaking.

For the last two years the average number of men employed on the
colony has been about 300, exclusive of the outside local labor which
it is necessary to employ during the fruit-picking season.

COST OF WORKING.

After paying administration expenses, there have been the following
annual deficits in the working of the colony:

1892	$22,445	1896	$25,465
1893	18,625	1897	3,550
1894	12,225	1898	4,275
1895	29,500	1899	6,895

A small grant per head from the general funds, on account of the
training of the newcomers during the probationary period, would
entirely wipe out the deficit of the last three years.

The fore shore and fishing section on the eastern extremity of the
colony is let to the fishermen of the Leigh village, and is a source of
steady income.

The operations of the Salvation Army here, as elsewhere, have been
productive of much good among the suffering and distressed of
humanity, and despite the almost insuperable difficulties that have
from time to time confronted the administration, the colony to-day is
in a flourishing condition.

Notwithstanding that year by year the working has shown a deficit,
the enterprise from a commercial standpoint can not be looked upon
as otherwise than a financial success, in view of the fact that the annual
deficit has almost reached vanishing point. Moreover, the aggregate
deficiency is more than counterbalanced by an enhanced value of the
land and colony generally.

THE MANAGEMENT OF THE COLONY.

To manage the colony the fittest are selected, irrespective of religious persuasion, provided there is evidence of a Christian tendency and proof of total abstinence.

Experienced men are at the head of each department. They report to, and take general directions from, the manager, who is resident on the colony.

The manager is assisted at the head office by a staff of officers who attend to the booking, correspondence, etc., under his personal guidance and direction.

In addition there is a properly equipped repairs section for effecting all necessary repairs on any part of the colony, and a traffic department which conducts all traffic, whether by road, rail, or water.

A citadel, or hall for public meetings, of commodious structure, is built inside the colony gates, for which rent is paid by means of free offerings by the men and attendants from the neighboring village and district. There are two spiritual officers in charge, who are supported in like manner.

All religious and semisecular meetings are held in this building and the men are expected to attend service at least once on Sunday either here or at some of the churches in the neighborhood. Special meetings are held every Saturday evening, more particularly for the benefit of the men, and one of the conditions of admission to the colony is that everyone must attend. They are usually of a semisecular character and are largely attended by residents in the vicinity.

Houses are provided in Castle avenue and in Orchard terrace for married men employed in the colony. There are also in Castle avenue a bakery and stores where every domestic commodity is obtainable at lowest market prices.

Farther along is a free library and reading room where a variety of excellent books, daily and weekly papers, and numerous magazines are provided for the men free of charge.

In close proximity is a blacksmith's shop where two smiths work at the anvil.

Lastly comes the house department, under the supervision of an officer whose duties are those of a superintendent and comprise catering for the men, control of kitchen and dining-room staff, dormitory orderlies, etc. He is furthermore responsible for the good conduct of the men after working hours, and is mainly responsible for the allocation of fresh comers to whichever department or section the capabilities and circumstances of the individual seem best to adapt him.

The superintendents of other departments have entire control of the men working under them, and from time to time make recommendations to the manager for an increase of remuneration to such of their men as are deemed worthy of advancement.   Under no circumstances can the minimum allowance which is to be paid in tokens, for the purchase of food, be reduced.   Industrious and energetic men speedily obtain the standard rate of outside wages with the additional advantage of full time.

AGRICULTURAL AND OTHER INDUSTRIAL ACTIVITIES.

Among the first efforts made in the farming section was stock raising, and in this the colony was singularly unfortunate for a succession of years.   So discouraging were the results that an abandonment of the experiment was seriously contemplated.   The misfortunes were chiefly in the form of abortions—this was the case almost without exception. Consequently, there was the somewhat serious loss of the young stock, coupled with the deteriorated value of the cows, which for conscientious reasons could be disposed of only to the butcher.   The best available skill was procured, which resulted in an extraordinary manifestation of diverse opinions.   The malady was attributed to the food, the water, the atmospheric and other influences, as well as to the bull, yet no remedy was discovered, though strangely enough the phenomenon disappeared as mysteriously as it came, and excellent cattle are now being bred.

Efforts to raise various breeds of sheep have been made and are being continued, with little hope, however, of forming a flock, owing to the unsuitability of the soil.   Ewes in lamb are bought and after one dropping are sold.   If kept longer they get poor.   The policy is to buy a flying flock in spring and sell before the trouble begins— thus clearing all out the second year.   It is by this means that such a large tract of pasture land can be utilized in a profitable manner.

In commencing operations in the cultivation of market-garden produce every conceivable obstacle was encountered.   Sour unfertile soil, overrun with weeds, unskilled and unwilling workers, scarcity of water, and a variety of other difficulties were met.   A commendable achievement, therefore, is the great expanse of standard fruit trees planted 7 or 8 years ago, and not yet in full fruit bearing, to which additions are still being made.   These, together with the vast rows of gooseberry, black currant, strawberry, raspberry, and other fruit-bearing bushes, as well as the immense vegetation which covers the extensive orchards, entirely dispel the misconceived notion that Kent alone could grow fruit and that Essex soil was incapable of producing anything but wheat.

An early class of potatoes is largely grown.   These are put on the first market and realize top prices, this of course necessitating buying from neighbors or others later in the season, but at much lower prices, the large quantity of potatoes required for consumption by the colony.

Poultry farming has been exceptionally successful. A few years subsequent to starting this industry the services of an experienced breeder were secured, and the results have been phenomenal. Apart from the large quantity of eggs sent away at high prices numbers of birds are bred each season, and they have been crossed to such a degree of perfection that specimens exhibited at all the principal shows and exhibitions throughout the United Kingdom have invariably won first, second, or special prizes.

This led to Her Majesty the Queen becoming a purchaser. The Right Hon. Cecil Rhodes was also an extensive buyer of the best poultry of the colony for his South African homes.

After various attempts at breeding, it was at last found that the land favored principally a "Yorkshire" pig—middle white—and in the development of this stock excellent results have been obtained.

The inconvenience and loss caused by a scarcity of water is now at an end. An artesian well has been sunk which will give a sufficient supply for all the colony's industries and for kitchen and cattle sheds, in addition to making provision for a very large supply on the market garden. It is probable also that the water will be conducted to the village of Hadleigh, and produce increased income.

The three brickyards, each yielding a distinct class of brick, are practically inexhaustible. The efficient and economical working of two of the brickyards is now completely accomplished. One is capable of turning out 80,000 bricks a week all the year round, at a net profit of not less than $2 per thousand. As the output of the other, 2,000,000 bricks were sold last season, and netted a profit of $1.50 per thousand. The output will not diminish, but will largely increase, while the net profit is almost sure to increase.

With the remaining brickyard a variety of complications have from time to time presented themselves, but this also gives promise of excellent results with the completion of certain experiments, which were rendered necessary in the application of modern machinery to the treatment of refractory clay. The average output on this yard will not be less than 50,000 a day, and the profit is estimated to be handsome. The process adopted here produces bricks of more than ordinary stability, which are in great demand for building bridges and other structures where the resistance of pressure is an essential element in the bricks. All three yards can not fail to be a lasting source of ever-increasing revenue, more than sufficient to meet any probable deficiency that may result in the working of either of the agricultural sections.

Other industries which were originally contemplated and started as likely sources of income were abandoned for economic reasons.

Chair making, for instance, could only be successfully carried on by the exclusive employment of skilled hands, which it was found next to impossible to secure.

Steam joinery was also abandoned in consequence of the location of the operations rendering the transmission of the manufactured article a much too expensive process.

A vigorous effort was made to breed rabbits, but it was unsuccessful and was abandoned.

Southend, a large town about 5 miles distant, is a ready market for the garden and farm produce of the colony. There is also a rapidly growing demand for these commodities in the immediate neighborhood. Thus is secured a quick sale at better prices than if the produce were sent to London.

Most of the bricks are sent to London by barge from the wharf of the colony, or by rail.

It has been presumed that the colony has taken advantage of supposed cheaper labor, and undersells competitors. That the labor is not really cheap has already been demonstrated. As for underselling, the colony's produce invariably commands the highest prices in the market. This is partly due to the fact that experienced salesmen are employed, and also to the fact that the best products of all kinds that can be secured are taken into the open market and sold at the best prices available.

The sales of the various products amounted last year to about $125,000, and could be increased, with an increasing rate of profit, by the introduction of sufficient working capital.

SUGGESTIONS FOR FUTURE DEVELOPMENT.

An industrial home for boys would be a great boon to the colony, inasmuch as it would remove or counteract one of the greatest difficulties with men, the majority of whom leave as soon as they become useful. The boys might be committed to the care of the colony for a definite period and so long could be relied upon for their labor. A subsidy from the Government might be granted for educational and other purposes. This home could be erected for $50,000.

Any number of the aged poor might be boarded out in suitable homes, and contributions sufficient to maintain them made by the poor-law authorities. Suitable labor, such as poultry rearing and flower cultivation, could easily be provided and their earnings would go to swell the revenue. Fifty such houses would cost about $50,000.

A valuable and remunerative extension of existing brickyards would cost about $25,000.

Extension of the railway to the highlands of the colony would mean an outlay of commendable wisdom ($25,000).

14453—No. 48—03——2

For want of the necessary capital there are still considerable tracts of land undeveloped, besides large tracts of land on the higher levels adjacent to it which ought to be acquired for extension of future operations, so as to afford greater facilities for a more successful manipulation of sheep and other stock, the higher levels to be in working in winter and the low lands in summer. To acquire this additional land and develop that already owned would require $30,000.

There is a range of hilly land running along the center of the colony upon which there are no made-up roads, although it would be quite possible to construct them. A good road here would add considerably to the value of the stretch of land which fringes the bottom of the hills and would materially enhance the value of the two adjacent brickyards. On such a road and on one or two main roads through the colony it would be a profitable investment to spend, say, $25,000.

For the use of the colony and for general water conveyance, six new barges should be acquired at a cost of $25,000.

Increased cottage accommodation for workers on the colony should be constructed at a cost of $10,000.

An excellent and safe investment would be in building workmen's houses at the eastern extremity of the colony, near the village of Leigh, a rapidly growing place, with railway station, 45 minutes from London. The outlay on such a scheme should be about $50,000.

Greenhouses for early fruit cultivation should be built at a cost of $25,000.

The stock of sheep and cattle might with advantage be increased by an outlay of $10,000.

The advantages of an installation of free power and light it is next to impossible to overestimate. The saving effected in the manipulation of present operations on the brickyards alone would be enormous. The dissemination of such power throughout the estate would effect economy in every direction. The light would be a lasting boon. Such a plant could be furnished at a cost of about $30,000.

When completed for the requirements of the colony the advantages of the plant might be extended to Hadleigh Village, which is close by, and thus become an additional source of income.

SOME CONCLUSIONS.

As a result of close observation, and the experience of some years' work among the classes designed to be benefited by the scheme, the conclusion is reached that all and more than all that General Booth promised in his "Darkest England" scheme can be accomplished.

The following essentials to success are suggested:

1. A suitable estate with some natural wealth (agricultural, pastoral, mineral, etc.).

2. The employment of experienced and devoted men and women as overseers.

3. The work on a sufficiently large scale to carry the incidental supervising expenses.

4. Sufficiently large also to make the settlement interesting and lively, not a mere hamlet or group of houses.

5. The principles of all the business departments must be commercially sound.

6. The doors should be open to all—married or single, without respect to creed or nationality.

COLONIZATION OF NEW ZEALAND.

The first Government to undertake colonization on a systematic plan was New Zealand. From the year 1870, when Sir Julius Vogel sent to the agent-general in London to dispatch 50,000 settlers in six months, up to 1894, when the Advances to Settlers Act was passed and $15,000,000 voted for colonization purposes, the entire ground of the systematic employment and settlement of the working classes as self-supporting home owners has been covered with sagacity and enterprise.

In one case a vast estate comprising 84,000 acres was bought back from its owner, resurveyed, and divided up into farms of from 50 to 100 acres and grazing farms of from 500 to 3,000 acres. One chief township and three villages were marked out with 2,000 acres near the central town site for suburban and garden lots. In 1892 the entire population of the estate consisted of one family and its attendants. In 1898 the population had increased to more than 1,000. The farms had been eagerly taken up and were paying the Government $5\frac{1}{2}$ per cent on the net cost, besides yielding the owners a good living.

Other large estates have been similarly bought back and settled by the Government, to the mutual satisfaction of the land owner and the settler.

The bold and generous policy which has been pursued by the New Zealand Government has many remarkable features.

In the first place, the married man with a family is given a distinct preference to the single man. Instead of marriage being discouraged, families broken up, and the single man, for false reasons of economy, given the preference, the exact opposite is the case. The married settler takes root more readily, is not liable to leave his farm, and is supplied with an abundance of unpaid and energetic labor. Again, the man without land is given the right of way in preference to the man who already has a farm in some other locality. This is in remarkable contrast to the "robbing Peter to pay Paul" plan pursued by our own railways and land-owning interests, which has stripped New

England of its best farmers to colonize the Middle States and which is now denuding the Northern and Central States to colonize the West and South.

Applicants for land in New Zealand are put through a rigid examination, and if it is found that they have farms elsewhere they are denied the privilege of occupying Government lands. The man who has neither land, money, nor experience in farming is carefully "shepherded" by the Government, is placed on road making, forest clearing, and general land improving, till he has gained the necessary knowledge, and is then helped to become a permanent settler and home owner. Under this enlightened tutelage the very tramp becomes in a few years a taxpayer, and even during the preparatory chrysalis stage meets all the expenses of his transformation, without being brought into competition with outside labor.

Mr. Lloyd thus summarizes the work of these "improved farm settlements," whose special object is the systematic employment and training of the out-of-works, for whose benefit civilization has elsewhere provided nothing better than "poorhouses, jails, and potter's fields:"

There are 45 of these improved settlements. They cover an area of 73,320 acres. There were on them, at the last report, 513 land holders and 1,854 residents. The settlers had cleared 15,141 acres of the bush and had grassed 20,814. They had been advanced $286,645, while the total value of the improvements which had been made by them was $420,840, and they have paid in rent and interest $13,210 yearly.

The farm laborer, who has been brought up on the land but has never had an opportunity of owning any, is wisely helped with the necessary advances which enable him to become a home owner.

The family which possesses a small amount of capital meets with abundant encouragement. Careful inquiries having been made as to their probable requirements and previous experience, they are assisted in obtaining the kind of farm on which they are likely to obtain the best results, and the improvements that their own capital enables them to make can afterwards be supplemented by the loans which they can obtain under the Advances to Settlers Act.

In addition to the settlement of farm lands, this act enables the workingman in the town to acquire suburban lots and gardens in the neighborhood of his work.

The loans granted by the Government can be either on the installment or on the fixed-loan system. On the installment plan mortgages are repayable by 73 half-yearly payments of principal and interest combined. These amount to only £3 ($14.60) per half year on each £100 ($486.65) advanced, thus placing the payments within easy reach of the settler.

On the fixed-loan system mortgages may be granted for any period not exceeding ten years, the principal being repayable at the end of the term.

Interest is charged at the rate of 5 per cent, reducible to 4½ per cent, provided payment is made not later than fourteen days after due date, and there are no arrears.

No loans are granted for less than £25 ($121.66) or more than £3,000 ($14,599.50). After not less than one-tenth of the loan has been paid, it may be readjusted, thus allowing further elasticity to the act. The loan may, morever, be repaid in whole or in part on the due date of any installment.

CANADIAN COLONIZATION.

While the Canadian Government has not at present adopted the New Zealand methods of colonization in their entirety, it has gone considerably beyond the ordinary American policy, inasmuch as there is an organized department for the purpose of promoting immigration, considerable sums of money being expended in the employment of agents, distribution of literature, and in definite efforts to turn the tide of immigration in the direction of the agricultural districts of Canada.

According to the annual report for 1901 the total number of immigrants for the year amounted to 49,149, of whom 17,987 went from the United States. In his report to the Canadian Government, Mr. W. J. White, inspector of agencies in the United States, says:

Since 1897 an active propaganda has been established and year after year has shown marked increases in the number of settlers who have gone to western Canada. The past year has been the most gratifying of all, exceeding anything that had been anticipated.

It is no longer the man with limited capital who comes to Canada, but the one who has, in many cases, a large bank account to his credit. It is no uncommon thing to see colonists filling a large train with their effects, going to Canada and settling in districts by themselves, quickly surrounding themselves with every social comfort and making not only their own settlement attractive, but adding value to the lands which surround it.

The American settler brings with him an experience which makes it very easy for him to soon get a return from the land which he has occupied, the usual difficulties of pioneering proving no obstacle to him. They at once have schools established, churches erected, and cause villages to spring up very quickly. The thousands of Americans who have made their homes in Canada during the past 5 years have all proved good citizens.

The reports of the agents show that 3,024 persons migrated during the year from Michigan, taking with them 93 carloads of stock and effects. From Wisconsin more than 500 persons migrated, taking with them a total of over $500,000 worth of property. One hundred settlers from Indianapolis, where the agency has only recently been established, took with them nearly $100,000 worth of property. From Nebraska 1,661 settlers migrated, taking 154 carloads of settlers' effects and a capital of $1,762,000. From South Dakota about 1,000 persons migrated, with 216 carloads of effects. From North Dakota 2,203 settlers migrated, with 354 carloads of goods and $307,000 worth of effects, besides personal capital. A very large migration also took place from Minnesota—2,060 farmers, 241 carloads of effects valued at $323,800, and a cash capital of $2,273,000.

The methods adopted with so much success by the Canadian Government to promote immigration are:

1. The location of agents at suitable centers.

2. The distribution of an enormous quantity of advertising matter, amounting during the last year to 1,193,000 copies, and including atlases and full particulars regarding the districts which it is desired to colonize.

3. Exhibits of agricultural produce, which are taken to all the various county fairs, when lectures are given, literature distributed, and information supplied to would-be settlers.

4. The conducting of settlers to the land and advising them as to the best localities for settlement, thereby protecting them from being deceived by designing persons who are interested in the sale of land and who so often rob the settlers of their little savings and leave them in a state of destitution to go to the cities, because they have been stripped of their limited supply of capital.

It will be seen, therefore, that while the Canadian Government does not go so far as that of New Zealand, and has no system of "advances to settlers," it has an intelligent and well-organized plan for the systematic colonization of persons possessing a small amount of capital, for guiding them to the best locations, and for protecting them against the depredations of land sharks.

The Canadian Government also assists in the establishment of creameries, providing the necessary capital, where the supply of cows in the neighborhood justifies the same. Its agents speak enthusiastically in regard to the success of the plans which have been adopted and as to the future prospects of the same.

COLONIZATION OF IRRIGATED LANDS.

Irrigation is a means to an end, and that end is colonization. Upon the rapid and complete occupation of irrigated lands by a sturdy and aggressive community of small farmers the success of great projects of colonization must ultimately depend.

To colonize promptly and effectively the lands which are to be irrigated it is not necessary to wait for the ordinary inflow of farmers possessing capital. The vast aggregations of labor in our great centers of population should be utilized. That this is feasible has been demonstrated.

The farm colonies of the Salvation Army were organized in 1898 to prove the possibility of relieving the congestion of the great cities, by removing worthy but poor families, furnishing them with the necessary capital, and settling them as home owners upon the land.

It was argued by those who, while friendly to the scheme, doubted its practicability, that (1) they would not go, (2) they would not stay, (3) they would not work, and (4) they would not pay. Four years of patient experiment have served to prove that these objections were groundless. The worthy poor of the great cities have gone, have stayed, have worked, and have paid. As a result of their successful toil they have become home owners, and the percentage of failures has been much smaller than was anticipated. Not only so, but thousands more would have gladly settled had the necessary capital been available.

The difficulty has not consisted in the lack of settlers. Suitable families by thousands are ready to move. Nor, again, has it been the lack of land. Millions of acres have been obtainable on the most reasonable terms. The great stumbling-block has been the paucity of capital available for carrying on the work. It has come in driblets, and has required to be spread over a considerable area and a long interval of time. Had the funds been available for operating on a larger scale with a sufficiency of capital, far more satisfactory results would have been obtained.

That colonization is practicable, where the farmer or settler has capital of his own to invest, has never been denied; hence the strenuous efforts of the West and South to obtain from the Eastern and Central States settlers who have money. The prospect of acquiring cheaper and more fertile land has in some cases led to the wholesale abandonment of entire districts which were once prosperous and might have remained so.

Now, if the farmer with a small amount of capital can accomplish such remarkable results in settling up and developing new lands, why should not the farm laborer, or the sturdy toiler of the city, who has no capital, achieve similar success, if the necessary capital be provided from an outside source? There are many things in his favor. His habits are usually more economical than those of the farmer with a little capital. His children are willing to help in the fields, and do not crave an expensive college education. The cheap, intelligent, and industrious labor of his family is far better than the unsatisfactory and hired labor on which the other usually depends. The small size of his farm enables him to cultivate it intensively, while the nearness of the various homesteads enormously increases the value of his land, and thereby automatically duplicates the result of his toil. His payments for interest are also smaller.

For instance, 1,000 acres occupied by 10 families in lots of 100 acres each will probably produce less than half as much as the same thousand acres occupied by 50 families in lots of 20 acres each. But, even granting that the produce should be the same, the real estate value would be enormously enhanced by the fact that in the former case the population would amount to about 50, and in the latter to 250. Hence the 20 acres of the small farmer would in a few years be worth more than the 100 acres of the larger holding, while the interest charges and payments for hired labor would be proportionately less.

This rapid increase in value of land thus thickly settled serves as ample security for the capital invested, provided that the management be honest, capable, and fairly economical.

Land bought four years ago at $25 is selling to-day as high as $100, while town-site land has been sold at a rate equivalent to more than $3,000 an acre.

Hence, so far from colonization being a risky enterprise, when carried out under proper auspices, it affords a maximum of security with a minimum of risk.

It will be invariably found that where colonization has failed it has been due to avoidable errors. For instance, from false motives of economy single men have been preferred to married men; small families, or none at all, to large ones. Or, again, the ownership of the farm has been refused, or communistic principles have been adopted. The majority of failures have been due to unpractical ideas. Everybody has owned everything in general, and nobody has owned anything in particular. Hence the industrious have not received the proper reward of their toil, have become discouraged, and have retired; while, left to themselves, the shiftless and unproductive have soon shipwrecked the most promising enterprises.

Again, in many cases no care has been exercised in the choice of colonists, or they have been handled harshly, suspiciously, and without sufficient tact or energy.

In other instances the enterprise has languished for lack of capital or owing to the absence of judicious oversight.

Indeed, the wonder is that in view of the general absence of system the results have been on the whole so remarkable in the occupation of vacant lands. But the time has now come when scientific colonization must take its place alongside scientific agriculture. The causes of failure must be ascertained and avoided. The principles must be discovered and followed which will insure a maximum of result with a minimum of risk.

As already stated, the Salvation Army is now operating three colonies in America—one in California, one in Ohio, and one in Colorado. About 400 persons have been settled upon some 3,000 acres of land. The families are entirely self-supporting. Some of them have paid for their holdings. Many of the 20-acre farms are valued at from $2,000 to $5,000. On some of them stone cottages and barns have been erected. But interesting and successful as has been this experiment, it is not necessary to rely exclusively upon the data thus furnished. A far larger and more extensive effort, already discussed to some extent in this article, has been made by the New Zealand Government. While others have been talking or dreaming, the enterprising Government of New Zealand has been acting and laying down lines which will undoubtedly be followed before long by the leading nations of the world.

The expenditure of $15,000,000 by that country upon the colonization of lands has been conducted on a system which leaves but little to be desired. The small driver who is being crushed by exorbitant interest, and driven to sell his farm or abandon it and turn to the city, can in New Zealand borrow money from the Government at 4½ per cent and repay it in thirty-six and one-half years, or sooner, if he desire. This checks the exodus from the country to the city.

The farm laborer who wants to become a home owner can buy land from the Government and borrow money at the same low rate of interest and on the same easy terms of repayment. This serves as check No. 2 to the abandonment of the country for the city.

The artisan or clerk in the city who wants to buy a farm and own a home can have his savings supplemented in the same generous manner.

If he prefers to have a cottage and a garden near the city, he can borrow for this purpose and build himself a home near his work, thus supplementing his wages by his garden produce and preparing for the evil day when he may be thrown out of work.

If he is stranded in the city and can not get work, the Government, instead of committing him to a semipenal pauper institution sends him into the country to make roads and improve some part of the national estate. He is paid wages, part of it in cash for his support and part of it in getting into shape a tract of land which is to become his future home, and on which he can, in due time, obtain from the Government a loan for improvements. His family, if he has one, is brought to him, and he is charged with the expense. If he has none, he is encouraged to marry and settle down. In this way nearly 50 industrial colonies have been established, and thousands of acres of land occupied.

Not a dollar has been lost by the Government, and while other nations are sinking millions upon their poor in useless waste, and never dreaming of recovering a cent, New Zealand is borrowing at 3 to 3½ per cent, lending at 4½, and settling its lands with taxpayers by means of those who would ordinarily be a burden on its revenues.

This interesting experiment in sociology has been going on for some ten years with complete success; and there seems absolutely no reason why, *mutatis mutandis*, the system should not be adopted in this country and throughout the civilized world. It would mean not only the settlement of our unoccupied lands, but the reoccupation of our abandoned farms by a thrifty, industrious population who would yield a rich revenue to the taxgatherer. Such a policy breathes the very essence of Christianity.

Important as has been the question of colonization in the past, it assumes double significance in view of the immense strides that public sentiment has recently taken upon the question of irrigation. The vast works that are now being planned and will shortly be constructed make it important that prompt and regular returns should be insured for the capital about to be expended by the speedy and systematic occupation of the lands thus opened for cultivation. It is the small farmer who is especially needed for the occasion, and it will be found that wisely guided colonization will prove a most valuable handmaid to irrigation.

Everyone who has had any experience in the question is aware that the one discouraging feature in irrigation has been the slowness with which the lands have been occupied on the usual voluntary principle of settlement by farmers possessing a small amount of capital. The heavy expenses connected with the upkeep of canals and reservoirs make it imperative that the land should be occupied with the utmost celerity. Otherwise the charges for irrigation, falling on the few, become extremely burdensome, if not impossible, alarming prospective settlers and effectually preventing, or at least greatly retarding, the work of settlement. Moreover the investors in the enterprise, not receiving any adequate dividends, are discouraged from advancing the additional capital necessary for the development or upkeep of the project.

It was pointed out to a prominent capitalist, who was president of one of the leading irrigation companies, that if it was worth while spending $2,000,000 in placing water on the land, it would surely abundantly repay the company to spend at least twice that sum in placing colonists upon it. But, strange to say, these men of intelligence, who had laid out vast sums in perfecting their water supply, were unwilling to "risk" a dollar in supplying capital for the colonization of their land.

Colonization as the handmaid of irrigation will bring within the reach of the latter new confidence and possibilities, while irrigation will prepare for colonization new realms of possibility, and these combined sciences will open before the working classes of this country new vistas of help and hope, will recreate that bulwark of national prosperity, the small farmer, and will provide an immense home market for our productions, making it easier for the masses of our population to be and do good, and to fulfill the obligations of citizenship and the dictates of God and conscience. Thus we may well hope that in solving the problems of poverty the bulwarks of national prosperity may, with the blessing of God, be strengthened and maintained, the dangers of class discord be minimized, and the harmonizing influences of religion be extended.

The
Salvation Army
in the
United States

By
Commander Booth Tucker

The Salvation Army in the United States

Christmas, 1899

The Salvation Army
Printing and Engraving
Department,
New York City.

THE SALVATION ARMY is the evolution of two great ideas—first, that of reaching with the gospel of salvation the masses who are outside the pale of ordinary church influences; second, that of caring for their temporal as well as spiritual necessities. In the one hand, it has carried to the people the Bread of Life, while in the other it has borne to them the bread that perisheth.

In July, 1865, the banner of this Army of Redemption was first unfurled in the East End of London, in a disused Quaker burial ground, by its founder and general, William Booth. In 1872 the first shot was fired on American soil by one of its converts, an emigrant from England, and in 1881 the work was regularly inaugurated by a band of Hallelujah Lasses under the leadership of Commissioner George Scott Railton.

If it were possible to put into figures the sum total of the indirect influence of the Salvation Army on religious thought and sociological progress, and could we add to this its direct and visible accomplishments, the result would indeed be startling. Apart altogether from the latter, there can be no doubt that an immense impetus has been given to the cause of Christ and philanthropy by stirring up thousands who have never entered its ranks to work of a similar character. Not only so, but a very large proportion of its converts have joined the churches and thousands of those who have been trained in its ranks are now occupying prominent ministerial and similar positions.

It is, however, with its direct operations that we are at the moment concerned, and these we have endeavored to describe as far as possible *pictorially*, with a view to presenting the subject in as concise and interesting a manner as possible.

Consul Mrs. Booth Tucker.

General William Booth
Founder of
The Salvation Army.

Commander F. de L. Booth Tucker.

Memorial Hall, New York City.

The
Salvation Army
incorporated
as an
American
Institution.

THE INCORPORATION of The Salvation Army in America under the laws of the State of New York places an official imprimatur on its organization and methods. Under this charter The Salvation Army becomes a legal entity and takes its place among the national institutions of the country.

The military system of its government, so essential to its success, remains unchanged, and at the same time ample powers are provided for the prosecution of the various branches of its religious and philanthropic work.

In preferring to incorporate under the laws of the State of New York, which are noted for their strictness, rather than under those of some other State where more latitude is allowed, it was believed that greater confidence would be created in the Army's stability and in the national character of its organization.

Nothing could have been more cordial than the reception granted to the Army's representatives by the members of the Legislature. The good work already accomplished was generously recognized by all parties, who united in facilitating the passage of the Act, and in exempting from taxation both our religious and benevolent operations.

AMERICA is a country in which the church and the Sunday school flourish as perhaps in no other country in the world; certainly its Sunday scholars outnumber those of any other country. And yet the problem of churchlessness is staring us in the face year by year with increasing seriousness.

The census of 1890 showed that church accommodation had been provided for 43,000,000 out of a total population of 60,000,000. This was an admirable proportion. But the fact cannot be denied that more than half the places of worship are thinly attended. It would be a generous allowance to say that 30,000,000 persons regularly availed themselves of the opportunity afforded. In other words, excluding infants, more than 20,000,000 persons habitually absent themselves from places of worship.

Go into the streets of any large city at the hour when every church throws open its door, and compare the number of people in the streets and parks with those who are at worship and it will be found that they number at least two to one.

Again, look at the religious census of our cities. Here is one with a population of 25,000. Its churches contain accommodation for about 5,000 (including Catholics and Jews). The majority of the churches are not more than half full—only a few of them being popular and crowded. The ministers will tell you they have no need of more churches; in fact, they dread the erection of a new building. And yet here are 20,000 persons who are neither provided for nor evince any desire to be so.

In the light of the above facts the extreme importance of the Army as a religious factor in our national life cannot fail to be recognized. Not only do tens of thousands of habitual neglecters of the ordinary means of grace make our services the only ones they ever attend, but we follow them to their open-air resorts, and by means of our street parades, music and open-air meetings, we bring the good news of salvation to their very doorsteps.

The spiritual operations of the Army in the United States include

667 Senior Corps or Posts,
545 Junior Corps or Posts,
21 Slum Posts,
27 Outposts.

At these centres upwards of 12,000 meetings are held weekly, between two and three million people being reached in the open air and indoors. From 35,000 to 50,000 persons profess conversion publicly every year, amongst them being thousands of drunkards, criminals and other outcasts of society.

It is impossible to exaggerate the value of the moral reformation thus wrought amongst the degenerate classes. Not that the work is by any means confined to them. Indeed, the bulk of our ordinary congregations is made up of the respectable working classes. No effort is, however,

Dormitory, "Ardmore" Shelter, Bowery, New York City.

Children's Home, San Francisco, Cal.

spared to induce every convert to go forth to the rescue of others. In fact the words Saint and Soldier are made to be synonymous. No sooner is the sinner saved than he is trained to systematic warfare and taught that his very soul's salvation depends on his becoming the saviour of others.

THE BLUE LAWS of Connecticut and other States show that at one time "the man in the street", was the exception, now he is the rule ; or, at least, whereas he represented a small and disreputable minority, now he represents a majority, including many of the most respectable classes. Anyway, he is there and can no longer be ignored. Nor can he be made religious by Act of Legislature.

True, we might leave him to himself and allow him to drift further on the downward course. We might abandon him to his fate. He has left the fold. He has himself to blame. We have many yet within the fold who need our watchful care lest they, too, stray. But that was not the policy advocated by the Good Shepherd. With ninety-nine in the fold, He would bid us seek the one lost sheep. How much more so when half the flock have wandered away !

Will they listen ? Oh, yes ! The one justifiable ground of complaint that the police sometimes bring against us is that the traffic has been obstructed by the crowds who gather on the sidewalks and roads and listen to the singing and the testimonies of our soldiers in the open air.

Oh, that crowd of soul-hungry, sin-bestained faces, the prodigal boys of a thousand homes, that group themselves around the ring wherever the flag of The Salvation Army has been hoisted ! They listen because they are talked to by ex-prodigals, who have tasted the bitterness of sin's cup. The tear in the speaker's eye, the tender tones in his or her voice, the song set to the exquisite popular melody which has swayed the nation's heart—how can they fail to awaken a responsive echo in that massive, thoughtful, silent throng ?

The anarchist and the burglar stand side by side with the merchant and the working man. The infidel's arguments die upon his lips. "If I were not an agnostic I should say it is Divine," is the testimony of one who voices the feelings of many.

Does the noise distress you? And yet you steel your nerves to the inevitable hurly-burly of a city's traffic. The former takes but one brief hour; the other commences with the dawn and reaches far into the night.

What about the drum? Why not? Thousands owe to it their salvation. Watch the wild boys of your streets running at its sound to catch up to the procession and forgetting their games and amusements while they listen to the gospel! You cannot force them to church with a rod nor attract them with a dollar, but here they come of their own accord and sacrifice their playtime for religion. The drunkard forgets his glass, the gambler his dice and cards.

And yet during the last year, in more than one city, attempts have been made to curtail our open-air liberties. Our very success in drawing together the godless crowds has been the excuse for the passing of ordinances which the Courts have over and over declared to be unconstitutional, and for the arrest of men and women whose only offence has been a passionate desire to win the prodigal and save the lost.

Happily the attempts thus made have been opposed by the united sentiment of the people and have resulted again and again in the vindication of our rights.

The most systematic and daring attack upon these valued rights was made during the past year in Philadelphia, where more than fifty of our officers and soldiers were arrested and in some cases treated with needless violence and indignity by the police. Our cause was ably advocated by ex-State Attorney Gordon and the arrests were declared to be illegal, resulting in a withdrawal of the restrictions which had been placed upon us.

A Sphere for Woman's Work. IN no religious or secular organization is there so free a hand allowed to women as in The Salvation Army, and to this fact is undoubtedly due a large measure of its success. The Hallelujah Lass has from the earliest days of the movement proved herself its Joan of Arc. Into the heart of slumdom she has carried the banner of salvation, and if her bonnet has become an

Workroom of the New York Rescue Home.

Our Chicago "Department" Store, where Secondhand Goods are sold to the Poor.

equally familiar sight in the offices of our merchant princes, it is only that she may plead the claims of the poor and champion their cause.

Problems that statesmanship and philanthropy have failed to solve have yielded to the gentle magic of these heroines of slumdom. " If there is a fight we make straight for the centre of it," said one of these girl warriors, who had been born and bred in the lap of luxury and had forsaken a comfortable home and brilliant social prospects in order to minister to the semi-savages of our city jungles. " Even if they are inflamed with drink or are using knives or revolvers, they never touch us. The people would almost tear them to pieces if they did."

" There are only two saloons in Chicago where we are not allowed to visit," said another of these officers, " and we go to them regularly every week. When the proprietor reminds us that he has already forbidden us to come, we answer, 'Yes, sir ; but we have come to see whether you have changed your mind yet!'"

Thousands of those who never cross the threshold of a church are to be found night after night in our meetings. Even when they do not profess to be converted, a marked change comes frequently over their lives. The meetings possess for these men a strange fascination, drawing them away from the glittering allurements of the saloons and dives and low music halls.

The personal magnetism of these women, their fearless face-to-face dealing with the wicked and their patient toil in behalf of the suffering poor are not the only secrets of their success. Prayer and faith equip the most timid of them for the platform duties from which they would naturally shrink. " It is so much easier," they say, " to act than to talk." And yet the burning words which fall from their lips, powerful in their simplicity, go straight to the hearts of their hearers and result in wonderful reformations.

As organizers and administrators many of our women officers have proven themselves to be in no sense inferior to the men, and the fact that they are equally eligible for our most responsible offices has helped to draw forth gifts which have only been latent for want of exercise.

T is sometimes alleged that "any man who wants work can get it." The magistrates and other public officials in the city of Brooklyn were recently asked the direct question as to whether this was so. City Magistrate Jacob Brenner replied as follows :

"I know of many men who are honest, sober and industrious, willing to work at anything and for any wages, who cannot find any employment. As a last resort many of these men, who are homeless, without shelter or food, apply at the Courts and are committed, often at their own request, to the County Jail, and even to the Penitentiary."

The above statement was endorsed by the following city magistrates: Henry Bristow, Charles E. Teale, William Kramer, Andrew Lemon, Alfred Steers and J. Lott Nostrand. Judge Teale says emphatically :

"It is not true that 'any man who wants it can get work,' and I know whereof I speak. There are hundreds of men, habits good, physically equipped for the hardest kind of work, willing to the point of anxiety to pitch into work without raising the question of compensation, who cannot obtain employment at any price. . . . The city magistrates, as a preventative and not a remedy or punishment, must take the very broadest humanitarian view and commit such unfortunates where at least soul and body may be kept alive."

The above opinions are endorsed by Deputy Chief of Police John MacKellar, by Chief Engineer C. C. Martin, and by Patrick Hayes, Warden of Kings County Penitentiary. The last of these gentlemen, who is absolutely in a position to know the actual facts, says :

"Men are constantly being committed here in large numbers who have been charged with no crime. Over fifty per cent. of the commitments to this institution are for vagrancy—the crime (?) of being 'out of work and homeless.' . . . By our treatment of the unemployed we are making criminals of men who have heretofore been honest, self-sustaining members of the community, and who *would be so again* could they obtain work."

The above statements are further confirmed by the returns of the labor unions for the State of New York. These show that during one of the most prosperous quarters ever reported upon,

Poorman's Hotel, San Francisco, Cal.

Chicago Waste Paper Depot.

ten per cent. of their members had been out of work. If such was the proportion amongst the powerful organizations represented, it is easy to imagine how great must be the suffering among the masses of unorganized labor.

In a single month during the past year The Salvation Army found employment in the United States for 4,780 of these workless persons, being at the rate of nearly 60,000 per annum.

With a view to providing work for the unemployed we have now eight Labor Bureaux and nineteen Salvage Brigades, Woodyards and Workshops. In addition to this, each of our Corps and Social Institutions is practically a Labor Bureau by means of which thousands of persons are annually found employment.

Our Salvage Brigades.

ONE of our most interesting and novel plans for finding work for the unemployed is the Salvage Brigade. This consists in the collection of waste paper, lumber, furniture, rags and clothing. The sale of these articles almost covers the cost of their collection and provides a large amount of unskilled labor which tides men over until they are able to find some regular employment. In the city of Chicago we have a contract for keeping several of the wards clear of waste paper. In some cities baskets are deposited with householders, our teams calling regularly to remove whatever articles may be placed in them.

The one difficulty that confronts us in extending this interesting and suitable method for dealing with the unemployed is that considerable expense is connected with the purchase of teams and baskets.

Salvation Junk Shops.

CONNECTED with some of our Salvage Brigades are Junk Shops where the old clothing, shoes and furniture we collect are repaired and sold to the poor at a low price. By this means quantities of cheap clothing are supplied at a nominal figure sufficient to cover working expenses, and at the same time avoiding the appearance of charity.

"WE could manage pretty well without food," said a converted hobo to me one day. "We became accustomed to the gnawings of hunger. But it was the awful longing for *sleep* that we could not endure. At first they would allow us to spend the night in the empty wagons and freight cars. That was bad enough. Many a morning have I woke up to find myself lying in a pool of water, drenched through to the skin, yet so exhausted that I had slept through it all.

"But after a time the police received orders to prevent us from using the carts or even the doorsteps. All night we would be compelled to keep moving. The longing for sleep at such times would be terrible. How thankful would we be to hide away in the corner of a lumber yard where the police could not find us!"

Our Shelters for the homeless poor have been greatly appreciated. Here, for ten cents a night, or for its equivalent in work, we have been able nightly to harbor thousands of destitute persons as well as to provide a clean and comfortable resting place for the multitudes of working men whose employment is irregular and whose wages are low.

The majority of these Shelters are on a self-supporting basis, the chief difficulty being the initial expenses for fitting up and starting them.

There are now forty-seven Shelters for men, with accommodation for about 4,800, and three for women, with accommodation for about 200.

Very interesting figures were obtained by officers relating to the nationality of visitors to a Salvation Army Shelter on the Bowery in New York. It was found on that particular night there were in the Shelter,

91 men of American birth,
14 German,
12 Irish,
8 English,
5 Swiss,
2 Swedish,
2 Scotch,
1 Austrian,
1 Canadian.

The Fresh Air Camp, Kansas City, Mo.

Children's Home, San Francisco, Cal.

**Blizzards
and
Winter Relief.**

I N ADDITION to the regular and systematic relief of poverty by means of its various institutions, The Salvation Army is able to render special service at times of great emergency.
During the prolonged blizzard of 1899, when for nearly a fortnight the railroads were tied up
and the streets were for some time impassable through the heavy falls of snow, some hundreds of
our halls throughout the country were thrown open to the poor by day and night. This was the
more necessary as it was impossible for many families who buy their fuel in small quantities to
obtain any supply. Thousands availed themselves of this relief.

Cent meals for the poor have also been a very popular form of assistance. For one cent a
pint of coffee and some bread have been supplied. A single member of a family could come and
fetch what might be required for a good meal at home, taking away as many cent meals as they
might pay for. This form of relief continued throughout the winter, and has already been
re-established this winter.

**Our Christmas
Dinners for the
Poor.**

D URING last Christmas we spread our tables throughout the United States for no less than
100,000 of our city poor. Next Christmas this vast number will probably be exceeded.
As a rule, the free distribution of food or clothing is discountenanced by us. The poor man
must either work or pay for whatever he receives. Nor do we find the slightest reluctance on the
part of the poor to fall in line with this reasonable request. We feel, however, that Christmas is
the one exception which must serve to prove the rule. On this occasion our doors are thrown
wide open and we welcome all who come.

Past experience having shown us that the most needy and deserving are often those who seek
to conceal their destitution and are unwilling to parade it before the public, we have made one of
our special features of Christmas Relief the distribution of Basket Dinners, each basket containing
sufficient for five persons. These are taken away by some member of the family and provide a
good Christmas at home, which is deeply appreciated.

Tickets for these basket dinners, as well as for the general public dinners, are carefully distributed through our officers and through the various religious and philanthropic agencies, so that the really needy poor are reached and helped.

For our next Christmas Dinner in New York the famous Madison Square Garden has been engaged. Basket dinners will be prepared for 16,000 and a general public dinner for 4,000. A mammoth Christmas Tree for children will also be provided on the Saturday previous to Christmas Day at our Memorial Hall in West Fourteenth Street.

The following are among those who have consented to act as Vice-Presidents and Patrons of the occasion : Commissioner John W. Kellar, President Board of Charities ; Edward Lauterbach, Esq., Counsellor-at-Law ; Hon. Chas. F. MacLean, Justice of the Supreme Court ; General Jas. O'Beirne, former Commissioner of Charities ; Countess Schimmelmann ; Hon. Bernard J. York, President Board of Police Commissioners, Greater New York.

Similar celebrations will take place throughout the country in all the principal cities. In Boston, Philadelphia, Chicago, St. Louis, Cleveland and many other cities from 4,000 to 5,000 persons are annually provided with Christmas cheer.

DOTTED up and down the leading cities of the world The Salvation Army operates nearly one hundred Rescue Homes for Fallen Women. During the twelve months ending 30th June, 1899, 5,132 of these daughters of sorrow passed through our Homes, from 70 to 85 per cent. of them being restored to lives of virtue.

In the United States we have now fourteen Homes, with accommodation for 360 girls, about 1,000 having passed through during the year, including preventive cases and some who only remained for a few days.

An interesting feature of this work is the organization of the girls who have left the Homes into a league known as the *"Out of Loves."* Occasional meetings are held for them at regular intervals, and they contribute as they are able to the expenses of the Home. One or two of the older Homes are now mainly supported by the contributions of the " Out of Loves."

Rescue Home, Boston, Mass.

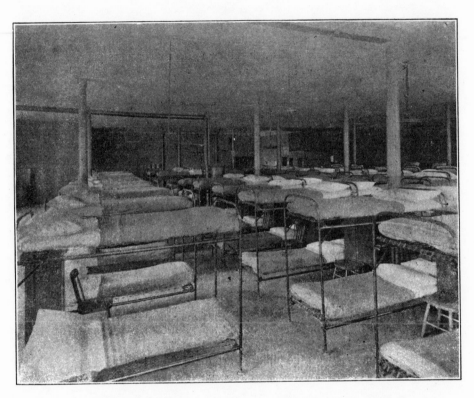

Dormitory, Central Workingmen's Hotel, Boston, Mass.

Work among Criminals.

MEETINGS are regularly conducted by permission of the authorities in many jails and penitentiaries, resulting in the conversion of many of the convicts. Upon their release from prison hundreds of ex-prisoners are assisted to find work and to return to the paths of honesty. Money is urgently needed to establish some regular Home for ex-criminals, similar to those which exist in other countries, through which 1,626 ex-convicts passed last year, resulting in about 80 per cent. proving to be satisfactory cases.

Our Work among the Children.

THE SERVICES of The Salvation Army have a special attraction for children. Whatever may be the opinion of the grown-ups as to the wisdom of our methods, there can be no doubt of their popularity amongst the young. Whether it be in the open air or in our halls, there is seldom any difficulty in arresting and retaining the attention of the children. This branch of our work has of recent years been carefully systematized and extended with the most encouraging results.

Perhaps the most interesting development has been the establishment of Brigades of Corps Cadets, consisting of boys and girls between the ages of twelve and eighteen who profess conversion and desire to be trained, with the consent of their parents, as future Salvation Army officers. The movement was started some two years ago in England and already numbers over 4,000 in that country. In America it was commenced at the early part of this year and now numbers about 400 members. The Cadets receive examination papers at regular intervals and are graded from time to time, besides being encouraged to go through a course of reading and assisting in the general corps work.

At the usual Junior meetings all the children are divided up into suitable classes and are carefully instructed in the Bible. A weekly meeting of what is termed the Band of Love arranges for the instruction of the children in various departments of useful knowledge.

A special book has been prepared by the Army for instruction in club drills, tambourine drills, flag drills, Chinese lantern drills, etc., accompanied with music and singing. These are extremely popular with the children. For the guidance of parents General Booth has written a valuable book on the training of children, and a special catechism suitable for them is now in the press.

In India, where only a small percentage of the population can read or write, the Army operates an extensive system of public schools, in which thousands of Hindoo children are educated. In a country like America this would, of course, be neither necessary nor advisable, and the fact is only mentioned to call attention to the spirit of adaptation which characterizes the Army work in all lands.

The Army, however, operates two very interesting Orphanages in the United States—one at Rutherford, near New York, and the other near San Francisco. It is hoped at an early date to greatly extend these operations, locating the children, as they grow up, on our various Farm Colonies, and thereby making them ultimately home owners.

Metropolis for Clerks and Artisans.

THE YOUNG MEN of our cities are surrounded with pitfalls and temptations. The honest young clerk or storeman struggling to keep up appearances on the small salary he receives, is liable to get amongst bad companions unless surrounded with a good, healthy, moral environment. Already several institutions of this character have been established, and there is a wide field for further advance. We shall be glad to hear from friends interested in this class of work and willing to invest some money in it, holding ourselves responsible for the regular payment of interest and the gradual repayment of the capital.

Our Work among Young Women Employed in Stores & Offices.

THE LOW WAGES paid to the thousands of young women employed in our large city stores is making it yearly more difficult for them to subsist. Homes, Hotels and Boarding Houses for respectable young women are being established to supply this urgent need at the earnest request of our friends and with their hearty backing.

119026

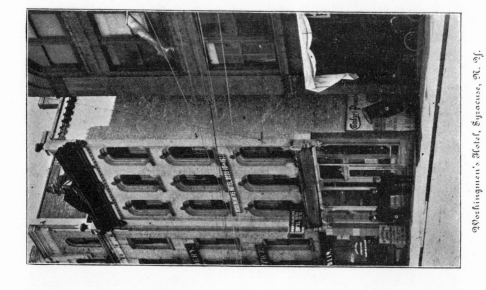

Workingmen's Hotel, Syracuse, N. Y.

Dining Room, Young Women's Hotel,
Boston, Mass.

Wood Yard, Waterbury, Conn.

Reception Room.

New York City Rescue Home.

Work Room.

Needless to say that in these Homes only women of thoroughly respectable character are received, and that they are run entirely distinct from our Rescue Homes. Owing to the fear that the one may be mistaken for the other we have sometimes found a difficulty in launching these institutions, but the early prejudice quickly disappears, and as soon as the Home is known it is usually crowded with a bright, intelligent class of young women who deeply appreciate the advantages and opportunities placed within their reach, many of them co-operating heartily with us in our plans for the betterment of others.

Farm Colonies. THE most alarming feature of our modern civilization is its wholesale disregard for and disruption of the family. Domicide is to the nation what suicide is to the individual. It is as false economy for society to destroy the *home* as it is for a man to blow out his brains so as to save the expense of feeding his body! And yet almost all modern pauperology is based upon the destruction of family ties. The consequences have been most disastrous and are bound to be increasingly so as time goes on.

Our cities are crowded with poor families who are reduced to the verge of starvation. The single man and single woman without any family responsibilities have a sufficiently hard struggle for existence. But their condition is as Paradise compared with that of the starving family.

"I have three brothers," remarked one of our Bowery boys, "but only one of them is *living*; the other two are *married!*" And yet beneath the jest what a pathetic world of suffering was hidden.

A very large proportion of these families have drifted from the country to the city from causes over which they have but little control. To return to the country other than as mere laborers is almost impossible. They have no capital with which to buy land or build homes or support their families till their crops are gathered. Moreover, in the cities they have always charity to fall back upon when their own resources fail. And yet there is no reason why the same charity which at present keeps them *in* the city at so enormous and unprofitable an outlay of capital should not bend its energies to removing them to the country and establishing them in cottage homes, of which they should become the owners.

It is now two years since our proposal for Farm Colonies was made public. During this period we have, though greatly crippled by the lack of capital, established three Colonies—one in Colorado, another in California, and a third in Ohio. The first of these is the most important, since upon it we have concentrated the bulk of our available capital, but the possibilities within reach of the other Colonies are almost equally great if the necessary funds should be forthcoming.

Each Colony consists of a tract of land divided up into small homestead farms with a cottage, from five to ten acres of land, a few cows, and some pigs and poultry. The colonist is assisted to get on to his feet, but has to repay all the money expended upon him, the amount being either repaid to the lender or reinvested in establishing another family.

On our Colorado Colony we have now about 150 men, women and children. With an outlay of about $30,000 we have been enabled to pay the first two instalments on the land, erect some twenty-seven cottages with outhouses of various descriptions, purchase about 150 cows, 75 horses, 120 pigs and 1,075 poultry, besides buying machinery, erecting a creamery and supporting the families of the colonists.

At the end of eighteen months what is the position of the Colony? Each family is able to meet its own expenses and has an excellent prospect of speedily repaying the few hundred dollars expended upon its establishment. The canteloupe crop has brought in a cash income of over $1,000, while the creamery brings a regular weekly income of about $50 to $60—say $2,500 a year. In addition to this is a considerable further income, which may be valued at not less than $1,000, from other vegetable produce and from poultry and eggs, pigs, etc. Large quantities of hay, alfalfa, corn and other produce for home consumption have also been grown by the colonists. Here, then, is a cash income of not less than $5,000 on an investment of $30,000, and this during the second year of the Colony's existence. Apart from this, moreover, is the great increase in the value of the land thus thickly peopled and intelligently cultivated. Unimproved land around our Colony has already increased from $22.50 to $50 an acre in selling value. The main line of

Central Food and Shelter Depot, Boston, Mass.

Workingmen's Hotel and Hall, Philadelphia, Pa.

the Santa Fe Railroad intersects our land, which is irrigated by one of the best canals in the valley of the Arkansas River, while we are able to obtain an abundant supply of water for drinking purposes within a few feet of the surface of our land.

Here, then, in our Colony system is a plan whereby the surplus population of our great cities may be removed *in families* by tens of thousands and converted from being the recipients of charity into self-respecting home owners. Doubtless the battle cry of the philanthropist and statesman in the near future will be, "The landless man to the manless land!" In other words, let the waste labor be placed upon the waste land by means of the waste capital and we shall thereby transform this trinity of modern waste into a unity of production.

For instance, let it be supposed that the $50,000,000 now consumed by our 3,000,000 submerged poor in our cities should be devoted to removing them on the above plan from the cities and placing them in homes of their own, what would be the result?

With this amount 500,000 persons could be taken in families from the cities each year and placed upon 1,000,000 acres of fertile land in cottages of which they would ultimately become the owners.

Within ten years the whole of this capital outlay would be refunded by them (interest having been paid on it in the meanwhile) and would be available for repeating the process until the balance between town and country had been restored. The natural increment of the land thus thickly populated would be an absolute security for the investment apart altogether from the industry of its occupants and the results of their labor, which would at least be abundantly sufficient to supply them with a living without their being dependent on the State or on private charity.

The relief thus afforded to the present strain upon taxes and philanthropy would be difficult to overestimate, while the self-supporting and self-respecting citizens thus created would enormously increase the home demand for the products of our great cities.

Few features of our philanthropic work afford a more interesting subject for the study and assistance of the benevolent than do these our Farm Colonies.

THE VAST NETWORK of spiritual and benevolent agencies established by the Army in the United States necessarily involves a heavy outlay of expenditure. This would not be possible but for the fact that each institution is placed upon a self-supporting basis and is taught to be responsible for its own expenses. Not only so, but each officer and soldier is trained to assist liberally according to his ability both in the support and extension of other branches of the work.

The main sources of income are the collections which are taken up at all meetings, both indoors and in the open air; the donations of friends of the movement, and the profits on the sale of " War Crys," books and uniform.

Officers are only granted a small salary sufficient to enable them to live in a strictly economical manner. They are, moreover, expected to meet their rent, gas, fuel and other liabilities before being entitled to draw their salary. At the same time, to supply their personal need, several funds have been established.

(*a*) The Sick and Wounded Fund provides two Homes of Rest, one near New York and the other in California, besides contributing towards the medical and resting expenses of officers.

(*b*) The Disabled Officers' Fund provides a regular weekly grant for officers who have been permanently disabled through disease or other cause.

(*c*) The Funeral Fund provides for the burial expenses of officers and their children.

To the above a fourth fund has now been added, known as the Officers' Dime Benefit League. Each officer will contribute ten cents on the death of a comrade officer, the amount thus raised being paid to the heirs or dependents of the deceased, or to such object as he may designate. The League includes two classes of members—beneficiary and non-beneficiary. The former will be restricted to officers, the latter will consist of friends and soldiers desiring to join the League. The maximum amount payable will be limited to $500, any surplus being credited to the fund, and, in case of accumulation, being paid over to the Disabled Officers' Fund.

Pittsburgh Workingmen's Hotel and Auditorium.

Workingmen's Hotel, Toledo, O.

It is needless to add that money is urgently needed for the extension of the various branches of our work here described. The opportunities that surround us are limited only by the fact that advances are dependent upon the necessary capital being forthcoming. Once established, the majority of our institutions are strictly self-supporting and find little difficulty in paying their *way*.

Regular balance sheets are published annually by the National Headquarters, while the accounts of every corps and institution throughout the country are carefully and systematically kept on forms specially provided for the purpose.

Nor are the funds administered without the most careful supervision and control of our ablest and most devoted officers, under the direction of regularly constituted councils.

The Board of Trustees established by the Act of Incorporation is responsible for the general administration of the funds and properties of the Army in the United States. The By-Laws drawn up under the Act further arrange for the establishment of a General Finance Council and a Property Council, each consisting of not less than six officers, who supervise the various details. Careful minutes of the proceedings are kept, and an annual return made to the Secretary of State, in addition to the publicatien of an annual report and balance sheet.

Further particulars may be obtained from Commander Booth Tucker or from the Legal Secretary, National Headquarters, 122 West Fourteenth Street, New York City.

Social Statistics. THE SOCIAL INSTITUTIONS of The Salvation Army in the United States now number 154, made up of

23 Food Depots;
54 Shelters, with nightly accommodation for nearly 5,500 persons;
23 Workshops, Factories and Labor Yards;
8 Labor Bureaux and Registry Offices;

3 Farm Colonies;
20 Slum Posts or Stations;
14 Rescue Homes for Fallen Girls, with accommodation for 360;
2 Homes for Waifs and Strays;

1 Missing Friends Department ;   1 Laundry ;

3 Hospitals and Dispensaries ;   11 Miscellaneous.

Four hundred and forty-two officers and employees are engaged exclusively in these Salvation Army institutions.

The returns for the Social work in the United States during one single month show the following interesting figures :

Institutions.	No.	Accommodation.	Beds Occupied.	Meals Supplied.	Found Work.	Officers.	Employees.
Shelters for Men,	49	5,311	131,426	....	1,610	63	135
Shelters for Women,	5	244	5,835	....	10	7	9
Food Depots,	23	....	....	27,424	....	..	..
Salvage Brigades and Wood Yards,	14	213	7,455	22,365	1,647	14	17
Labor Bureaux,	8	....	....	....	1,530	8	..
Farm Colonies,	3	202	....	....	....	18	..
Rescue Homes,	14	360	11,095	33,285	....	94	..
Children's Homes,	2	60	2,100	6,300	....	6	3
Hospitals and Dispensaries,	3	....	....	....	....	46	..
Slum Posts,	20	....	....	....	....	46	..
Missing Friends,	1	....	....	....	....	1	..
Miscellaneous,	12	....	7,070	21,210	....	21	..
Total,	154	6,390	164,981	110,584	4,797	324	164
Annual Rate,	..	2,253,600	1,836,000	1,300,000	57,000	..	..

Rescue Home, Cleveland, O.

Group of Slum Officers under Mrs. Lieut.-Col. Brewer.

**How to Help
The
Salvation Army.**

I. By taking a Mercy Box in your home and putting into it one cent a week for the poor.

II. By becoming a Mercy-Box Secretary and getting others to take a Box.

III. By helping us to place our Merchants' League Box in stores, restaurants and offices.

IV. By joining the Auxiliary League and subscribing five dollars a year (payable, if preferred, quarterly), when we will send you regularly one of our publications.

V. By loaning to our Colony or Building Fund any money you may have laid by, when we will give you good security and interest, and you will realize that your money is doing good, besides being safely invested.

VI. By representing our work to moneyed friends and urging them to assist us while living and to remember our work in their wills.

VII. By reading and circulating our literature.

VIII. By praying for us.

Addresses of Social Institutions for the Poor in the United States.

NEW YORK.

1. . National Headquarters, 120-124 W. 14th Street.
2. . Secretary for Farm Colonies (Col. Holland), 124 W. 14th Street.
3. . Secretary for City Social (Col. Holland), 124 W. 14th Street.
4. . Department for Missing and Lost Friends (Col. Holland), 124 W. 14th Street.
5. . Merchants' League, 120-124 W. 14th Street.
6. . Central Relief Office, 120-124 W. 14th Street.
7. . Labor Bureau, 120-124 W. 14th Street.
8. . The Ardmore Workingmen's Hotel, 83 Bowery.
9. . The Workingmen's Hotel, 21 Bowery.
10. . The Dry Dock Workingmen's Hotel, 118 Avenue D.
11. . The Glyndon Workingwomen's Hotel, 243 Bowery.
12. . The Rescue Home (for Fallen Women), 316 E. 15th Street (Stuyvesant Square).
13. . The Cherry-Tree Home, for Waifs and Strays, Rutherford, N. J.
14. . Slum Post 1 Hall and Slum Officers Training Home, 88 Cherry Street.
15. . Slum Day Nursery for Children, 88 Cherry Street.
16. . Slum Post 3, 63 Watt Street.
17. . Slum Post 5 in Hell's Kitchen, 532 W. 39th Street.
18. . Italian Corps, 21 Hester Street, Mulberry Bend.
19. . Penny Meal Depot, 88 Cherry Street.
20. . Slum Training Home, 88 Cherry Street.

BROOKLYN.

21. . Slum Post 1, 53 Columbia Street.
22. . Labor Bureau, 327 Atlantic Avenue.

JERSEY CITY, N. J.

23. . Workingmen's Hotel, 93 Montgomery Street.
24. . Industrial Salvage Depot for Homeless Men, 337 Newark Avenue.

BOSTON, MASS.

25. . Divisional Headquarters, 882-890 Washington Street.
26. . Old Central Hotel for Workingmen, 886 Washington Street.
27. . New Central Hotel for Workingmen, 886 Washington Street.
28. . Labor Bureau for Unemployed, 886 Washington Street.
29. . Public Reading Room, 886 Washington Street.
30. . Cheap Food Depot, 886 Washington Street.
31. . The Hub Workingmen's Hotel, 187-189 Hanover Street.
32. . The Unity Hotel for Men, 37 Green Street.
33. . The Hotel Benedict for Young Women, 20 Common Street.
34. . The Ladies' Lunch and Restaurant, 20 Common Street.
35. . Industrial Salvage Depot for Homeless Men, 394 Harrison Avenue.
36. . The Junk Store for Sale of Goods to the Poor, 394 Harrison Avenue.

Rescue Home, St. Paul, Minn.

Dining Room, Salvage Depot, Chicago, Ill.

BOSTON—Continued.

37..Wood-Yard, Rear 394 Harrison Avenue.
38..The Rescue Home, 147 Mount Pleasant Avenue, Roxbury, Mass.
39..Slum Post, 31 Athens Street, South Boston.
40..Slum Post, 48 Battery Street.

PROVIDENCE, R. I.

41..Workingmen's Bethel for Seamen, 98 Wicken-den Street.
42..Slum Post, 276 S. Main Street.

FALL RIVER, MASS.

43..Workingmen's Hotel, Rear 55 4th Street.

TROY, N. Y.

44..Divisional Headquarters, 25 King Street.

SYRACUSE, N. Y.

45..Workingmen's Hotel, 311 S. Clinton Street.
46..Food Depot, 311 S. Clinton Street.

ROCHESTER, N. Y.

47..Workingmen's Hotel, 38-40 Exchange Place.
48..Food Depot, 38 Exchange Place.

BUFFALO, N. Y.

49..Divisional Headquarters, Ellicott Square.
50..Workingmen's Hotel, 79 Main Street.
51..Food Depot, 79 Main Street.
52..Rescue Home, 390 Humboldt Parkway.
53..Slum Post, 35 Michigan Street.

BRIDGEPORT, CONN.

54..Workingmen's Hotel, 376 Water Street.

WATERBURY, CONN.

55..Workingmen's Hotel.
56..Wood-Yard for Unemployed, 212 Meadow Street.

OLEAN, N. Y.

57..Workingmen's Hotel.

BINGHAMTON, N. Y.

58..Workingmen's Hotel.

NEW BRUNSWICK, N. J.

59..Workingmen's Hotel.
60..Industrial Home for Men.

PHILADELPHIA, PA.

61..Divisional Headquarters, 14 South Broad Street.
62..Workingmen's Hotel, 8th and Vine Streets.
63..Workingmen's Metropole, 305 South Second Street.
64..Rescue Home, 5415 Lansdowne Avenue.
65..Maternity Home, 5415 Lansdowne Avenue.
66..Slum Post 1, 160 Lombard Street.
67..Slum Post 2, 705 Rodman Street.

PITTSBURG, PA.

68..Workingmen's Hotel, 340 Third Avenue.

BRADFORD, PA.

69..Workingmen's Hotel.

CLEVELAND, O.

70..Divisional Headquarters, 715 Garfield Building, Euclid Avenue.
71..Workingmen's Hotel, 86 Michigan Street.
72..Farm Colony, Fort Herrick, Willoughby, near Cleveland, O.
73..Rescue Home, 91 Kinsman Street.
74..Slum Post, 897 St. Clair Street.
75..Industrial Salvage Brigade for Homeless Men.

TOLEDO. O.

76..Workingmen's Hotel.

CINCINNATI, O.

77..Workingmen's Hotel, 27 Longworth Street.
78..Workingmen's Hotel, Vine and Canal Street.
79..Slum Day Nursery, Front Street.
80..Slum Post, 403 E. Front Street.

LOUISVILLE, KY.

81..The New Gun, Workingmen's Hotel, 342 W. Jefferson Street.

NASHVILLE, TENN.

82..Workingmen's Hotel and Food Depot, 170 N. College Street.

CHICAGO, ILL.

83..Divisional Headquarters, Dexter Building, 84 Adams Street.
84..Evangeline Workingmen's Hotel, 387 South Clark Street.
85..Food Depot, 387 South Clark Street.
86..Harbor Lights Workingmen's Hotel, 118 W. Madison Street.
87..Beacon Workingmen's Hotel, 515 State Street.
88..The Mina Women's Hotel, 54 Wabash Avenue.
89..Salvage Warehouse, 411 Harrison Street.
90..Junk Store, Where Goods are Sold to the Poor, State Street.
91..Labor Bureau, 566½ W. Madison Street.
92..Dispensary, 3761 Cottage Grove Avenue.
93..Rescue Home, 6201 Wabash Avenue.
94..Slum Post 1, 136 Pacific Avenue.
95..Slum Post 2, 171 Seber Street.
96..Slum Post 3, 82 W. 15th Street.

GRAND RAPIDS, MICH.

97..Rescue Home, 1230 South Division Street.

ST. LOUIS, MO.

98..Divisional Headquarters, 810 Olive Street.
99..Lighthouse Workingmen's Hotel, 9th and Market Streets.
100..Beacon Workingmen's Hotel, 11 Market Street.
101..Slum Post 1, 1303 N. 8th Street.
102..Slum Post 2, 424 S. Second Street.
103..Rescue Home, 3740 Marine Avenue.

SPRINGFIELD, ILL.

104..Workingmen's Hotel, 113 South 8th Street.
105..Food Depot, 113 South 8th Street.

LITTLE ROCK, ARK.

106..Workingmen's Hotel.
107..Restaurant.
108..Wood-Yard for Out-of-Works.

KANSAS CITY, MO.

109..Divisional Headquarters, cor. 13th and Walnut Streets.
110..The Metropole, cor 13th and Walnut Streets.
111..Workingmen's Palace, 211-213 East 5th Street.
112..Food Depot, 211-213 East 5th Street.
113..Summer Fresh Air Depot, 211-213 East 5th Street.
114..Penny Ice Depot, 211-213 East 5th Street.
115..Workingmen's Hotel, 351 Minnesota Avenue.

TOPEKA, KAN.

116..Hospital.

HOUSTON, TEX.

117..Workingmen's Hotel, 2014 Court Street.
118..Wood-Yard, 2014 Court Street.

AMITY, COL.

119..Farm Colony, P. O., Amity, Prowers, Co.
120..Farmers' Institue, P. O., Amity, Prowers C.
121..School, P. O., Amity, Prowers Co.

Day Nursery, "Rat Row," Cincinnati, O.

Workingmen's Hotel, Cincinnati, O.

DENVER, COL.

122..Divisional Headquarters, 2938 Lawrence Street.
123..Workingmen's Hotel, 1320 16th Street.
124..Food Depot.
125..Industrial Salvage Brigade for Homeless Men.

CRIPPLE CREEK, COL.

126..Workingmen's Hotel, 234 Meyers Avenue.
127..Food Depot, 234 Meyers Avenue.

OMAHA, NEB.

128..Rescue Home, 2015 Pinkney Street.

ST. PAUL, MINN.

129..Rescue Home, 666 Jackson Street.

SALT LAKE CITY, UTAH.

130..Workingmen's Hotel, 35 Franklin Avenue.
131..Food Depot, 35 Franklin Avenue.
132..Wood-Yard.
133..Laundry.

PORTLAND, ORE.

134..Divisional Headquarters, 620 Chamber of Commerce.
135..Workingmen's Hotel.
136..Rescue Home, 63 4th Street.

CLEVELAND, O.

Workingmen's Metropole.

NEWARK, N. J.

Workmen's Hotel, Washington Avenue.
Industrial Home for Men, Boyd Street.

SEATTLE, WASH.

137..Wood-Yard, Yester Way and 3d Avenue.
138..(Colby) Wood Camp.
139..Basket Factory.

SAN FRANCISCO, CAL.

140..Divisional Headquarters, 1139 Market Street.
141..Workingmen's Institute, 158 New Montgomery Street.
142..Food Depot, 158 New Montgomery Street.
143..Dispensary.
144..Wood-Yard.
145..Labor Bureau, 158 New Montgomery Street.
146..Women's Shelter, 603 Washington Street.
147..Food Depot, 63 Washington Street.
148..Rescue Home, Beulah.
149..Children's Home, Mills College, P. O. Cal.

SACRAMENTO, CAL.

150..Workingmen's Hotel, 115 K Street.

LOS ANGELES, CAL.

151 Young Women's Boarding Home.
152..Workingmen's Hotel, 759 Upper Main Street.
153..Rescue Home, 330 N. Griffin Avenue, E. Los Angeles.

ROMIE, CAL.

154..Farm Colony, Fort Romie, Monterey Co.

Since the copy for the above was sent to the printers the undermentioned Social Institutions have been opened and put into operation :

DES MOINES, IA.

Rescue Home for Fallen Women, 1314 West 35th Street.

SEATTLE, WASH.

Workmen's Hotel.

The Workingmen's Palace, Kansas City, Mo.

Divisional Headquarters, Hall and Metropole, Kansas City, Mo.

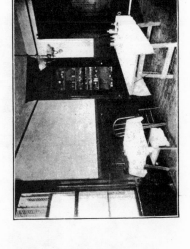

Corridor in the Metropole, Kansas City, Mo.

The Dispensary, Topeka Hospital.

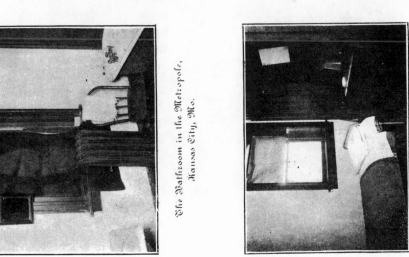

The Bathroom in the Metropole, Kansas City, Mo.

A Snug Room, Metropole, Kansas City, Mo.

Salvage Depot and Store. Boston, Mass.

Men Sorting Paper, Salvage Depot, Boston, Mass.

Rescue Home, Beulah, San Francisco, Cal.

Dining Room, Rescue Home, Beulah, San Francisco, Cal.

The Women's Shelter, San Francisco, Cal.

On the Verandah, Rescue Home, Beulah, Cal.

Penny Ice Wagon, Kansas City, Mo.

A Corner of the Rescue Home Dormitory, San Francisco, Cal.

Group of Girls at Work, Cleveland Rescue Home.

Workingmen's Hotel and Salvage Depot, Newark, N. J.

Workingmen's Hotel, Newark, N. J.

One of our Latest Developments.

Home for Working Girls, Boston, Mass.

Cherry Street Slum Corps Day Nursery, New York City. (One-cent Meals here.)

Dormitories, Cherry Street Slum Corps Day Nursery, New York City.

A Group of Slum Angels.

Workingmen's Hotel, Providence, R. I.

Farm and Cattle, Fort Romie, Cal.

Colonist's Cottage, showing Vegetable Garden, Fort Romie, Cal.

A Group of Colorado Colony Children.

Our First Stable on the Prairie.

Corner of Colorado Colony in early days.

Typical Colonist's Cottage, Colorado.

Colony Barnyard Scene.

Women at Work, Rescue Home, St. Paul, Minn.

BALANCE SHEETS

OF

THE SALVATION ARMY

1899

The Salvation Army.

NOTE.—The accounts as published herewith embrace only those funds which are handled and dealt with directly at the National Headquarters in New York City, and do not include contributions or disbursements of any of our 700 local stations, nor accounts in connection with any charitable or social work outside of New York City and the immediate neighborhood. Balance sheets are issued locally giving these particulars. The only exception to this is the Farm Colony accounts. The balance sheet for the half year ending September 30, 1899, has been added to those of the previous year, owing to the change of date in our financial year consequent upon the incorporation.

General Income and Expenditure for Year Ending March 31, 1899.

HEADQUARTERS GENERAL MAINTENANCE.

Dr.			Cr.		
To Rent of Headquarters and Staff Homes................	$14,664 35		By Donations and Auxiliary Membership Subscription Fees	$5,085 49	
" Repairs and Alterations, including Fittings for Offices and Officers' Quarters....	2,057 63		Less Expenses of Department, Stationery, Periodicals and 25 per cent. returned to Divisions....	3,131 28	$1,954 21
" Fuel and Light for Offices, Auditoriums and Water Tax	3,898 18				
" Printing and Stationery for Headquarters' General Work and Disposition of Forces	2,094 81		" Harvest Festival Demonstration. Total received at National Headquarters from all sources..........	15,296 43	
" Postage and Telegrams...	3,135 33		Less cost of Collections, Printing, Expressage, Postage, Labor and Commissions to Divisions..........	2,643 03	12,653 40
" Salaries of Headquarters and Employees...........	15,585 70				
" Legal Expenses, including Salaries, Stationery, Postage and Special Legal Charges in connection with Incorporation with Traveling Expenses.........	2,831 73		" Divisional Fund. Total Income, 10 per cent. on General Divisional Income...	2,605 82	
" Interest on Loans and Discount.............	1,582 84		Less portion applied on old Divisional Accounts......	880 33	1,725 49
" Expressage and Office Expenses, including depreciation on Furniture and Fixtures, Headquarters and Officers' Quarters...	5,053 84		" Transfer from Trade Department. Profit on Sales.		49,244 82
" Advertising and Appeals...	3,109 96	$54,014 37	Carried forward......		$65,577 92
Carried forward......		$54,014 37			

By Balance from Property department. Income and Expenditure Account.......

$153,009 20

Brought forward....... $54,014 37

To Grants to Corps and Divisions for Rents, Traveling and Special Operations....   11,791 21

" Staff Traveling Expenses of Officers visiting Divisional Centres for Special Demonstrations, Councils of War, &c......   3,211 48

" Divisional and Corps Special Expenses of Officers set apart for Special Evangelistic Work and Inspection of Corps....   4,176 56

" S p e c i a l Demonstration, Printing, Postage, Traveling, Rents, including Labor.   6,051 70

" Junior Soldier War, National Oversight, including Departmental Expenses and Traveling, &c....   2,076 35

" Training, Homes, National Oversight and Management Expenses, including Traveling, Grants, Rent and Clothing, Stationery and General Maintenance......   5,924 24

$33,231 54

" Naval and Military League, Rent of Halls and Tents, Traveling and Officers' Allowance......   1,707 73

" Less Income from Donations, Collections, &c......   1,122 04

585 69

" Sick and Wounded. Maintenance of Homes of Rest, Grants to Officers, &c......   2,874 55

" Less Collections and Donations   2,342 31

532 24

" Grants to City Social Operations and General Supervision......   11,411 74

" Balance carried to Salvation Army Fund.......   53,233 62

$153,009 20

Social and Relief Branches.

Income and Expenditure Account, March 31, 1899.

To	Social Department. General Maintenance and Expenses of Department, including Stationery, Traveling and Depreciation of Plant and Fixtures in Social Institutions...	$3,447 45	By	Collections, Donations and Traveling Expenses refunded, including Loans returned Grant from Mercy-Box account ... $1,788 12	
				600 00	$2,388 12
"	Salary of Staff and Employees of Social Department. Expenses of Central oversight of all Social Operations...	3,958 00	"	Institutions. Income from Charges for Beds and Donations—	
"	Investigation Department. Expenses of Department, including Salaries, Traveling, Postage, Stationery, &c. 1,062 03 Less Income from Subscribers ... 278 82	783 21		The Ardmore Shelter... 4,376 75 " Bowery " 4,794 42 " Dry Dock " 3,012 17 " Glendon " including Mercy-Box Grant... 3,084 01 The Jersey City Shelter. 3,818 68 " Newark 1,021 21	20,107 24
"	Institutions, Rent, Salaries and Maintenance Expenses— The Ardmore Shelter... 3,928 66 " Bowery " 3,926 68 " Dry Dock " 3,443 36 " Glendon " 3,084 01 " Jersey City " 3,960 67 " Newark " 1,168 42	19,511 80	"	Salvage Depots from Sales of Stock and Donations for Greater N. Y. Depot Jersey City Depot... 2,085 68 2,111 10 Newark ... 1,309 95	5,506 73
"	Salvage Departments. Rent, Labor, Maintenance, Salaries and Help— Greater N. Y. Salvage... 4,133 80 Jersey City " 2,087 06 Newark " 2,007 91	8,228 77	"	Rescue and Slum Work. Collections, Donations and Traveling refunded... 1,885 18 From Mercy-Box Account... 702 11	2,087 29
"	Rescue and Slums. General Maintenance Expenses of Department. Traveling, Stationery, Postage, Grants to Homes, &c...	3,049 33	"	New York Rescue Home, Including Donations, Collections and Inmates' Work, including Receiving Home..	666 16
"	Institutions for Rent, Maintenance, &c.— New York Rescue Home.. 1,446 97 N. Y. Receiving Home. 1,040 38	2,487 35	"	Children's Home (Cherry Tree) Donations, Collections and Special Demonstrations... 2,379 31 From Mercy-Box Account.. 463 57	2,842 88
			"	Maternity Home.........	116 00
			"	Slum Work Donations and Grant from Mercy Box..	415 16
	Carried forward......	$38,978 56		Carried forward.....	$34,129 58

(Continued)

	Brought forward........	$2,487 35	$38,978 56	
	Cherry Tree (Children's) Home	2,842 88		
	Maternity Home........	817 37		
	Slum Home.............	415 16	6,562 76	
				$45,541 32

	Brought forward........		$34,129 58
By	Balance to General Fund, Income and Expenditure Account		11,411 74
			$45,541 32

Special Relief Works.

To	Expenses of Department. Labor. Collecting on Streets, Carfare and General Supervision, including meals for Collectors.............	866 76		
"	Purchases of Permanent Collecting Material.......	446 52		
"	Printing, Postage and Advertising, Expressage, &c..	458 56		
"	Clothing, Shoes and Garments	220 26		
"	Lodging, Coal, Temporary relief in various Districts, and Employment........	2,308 06		
"	Cost of Christmas Dinner for Meat, Groceries, Bread &c..........	1,204 24	5,504 40	
"	Balance carried down.....		683 24	
			$6,187 64	

By	Collection on Streets and Donations..............	$6,187 64
		$6,187 64

Mercy Box Account.

To	Purchases of Stock, Stationery, Expressage, Postage, Salaries and Traveling, Commissions to Divisions..	$3,500 38		
		2,041 19	$5,541 57	
"	Grants to Children's Home.	463 57		
"	Slums........	238 17		
"	Rescue Homes......	702 11		
"	Womans' Shelter..	749 18		
"	Social General Account........	600 00		
"	Womans' Ministering League.	150 00	2,903 03	
			$8,444 60	

By	Total Collection Raised at National Headquarters.....	$8,444 60
		$8,444 60

Property Department.

To	General Maintenance, cost of Department, including Salaries, Traveling and Stationery		$2,030 54	By	Rents from Properties for Interest, Insurance, &c.		$15,144 38
"	Interest on Mortages		11,135 56	"	Properties Donated and Secured for Salvation Army purposes		87,926 54
"	Repairs to Properties		195 06				
"	Insurance on Buildings and Properties		329 76				
"	Depreciation in Sale of disused Properties. Valuation of Properties	$4,898 72					
	Realized from Sale	2,950 00					
	Depreciation		1,948 72				
"	Balance to General Income and Expenditure Account		87,431 28				
			$103,070 92				$103,070 92

Funeral Fund.

To	Payments for Funeral Expenses during the Year		$1,945 27	By	Balance reported April 1st, 1898		1,369 37
	Transfer to Sick and Wounded Fund and Maintenance of Home of Rest		1,500 00	"	Total Receipts at Headquarters from Divisions		2,976 92
		$3,445 27					$4,846 29
		901 02					
			$4,346 29				
"	Balance brought down		$4,346 29				$4,346 29

Disabled Officers' Fund.

To	Grants to Disabled Officers during Year ending March 31st, 1899		$2,264 48	By	Balance Reported March, 1898		$10,491 36
"	Balance carried down		10,968 88	"	Commission paid over from War Cry during year and Interest on Investments		2,742 00
			$13,233 36				$13,233 36
							$13,233 36

Balance Sheet for Year ending March 31, 1899.

LIABILITIES.

To	Loans on Mortgages, on Freehold and Leasehold Properties		$291,454 75
"	Collections for Building purposes. Deposited by Corps.	$5,892 86	
"	Sundry Creditors, various Loans and Trust Money, secured by Mortgages, Special Relief, Funeral Fund, Disabled Officers, Collection account, Armenian Special, Warriors' Min. League...	12,991 31	
"	Self-Denial, Balance carried forward, incomplete returns.	11,361 75	
"	Sundry International Accounts, for Missionary Fund, Loans for Officers Traveling, &c...	12,492 56	
"	Sundry Creditors, Loans for Fixed Periods, General Work...	23,000 33	
"	Sundry Creditors, Loans Colonization purposes......	19,895 00	85,633 81
"	Salvation Army Fund, March, 1898...	265,507 30	
"	Balance from General Income and Expenditure Account	53,233 62	318,740 92
			$695,829 48

RESOURCE.

By	Freehold and Leasehold Property, March, 1898.....	$476,255 89	
"	Addition during the year, including property donated.	133,549 65	
		609,805 54	
	Less Depreciation.........	1,948 72	607,856 82
"	Furniture and Fixtures, Headquarters and Officers' Homes, March 31, 1899..	11,996 79	
	Addition during Year.....	4,119 94	
		16,116 73	
	Less Depreciation.........	4,116 73	12,000 00
"	Sundry Debtors, Loans on Properties		2,252 07
"	Sundry Debtors, Loans to Divisions for General Extension and Social Advances		24,264 59
"	Furniture and Fixtures in City Social Institutions, reported March 31st, 1899.	7,500 00	
	Addition during Year......	4,824 93	
		13,324 93	
	Less Depreciation.........	1,532 49	10,792 44
"	Farm Colonies. Improvements on Land, and Instalments.....		24,481 23
"	Cash at Bank........		14,182 33
			$695,829 48

Trade Department

BALANCE SHEET FOR YEAR ENDING MARCH 31, 1899.

To	Capital, March 31st, 1899,	$61,463 72			
	Less Transfer to General Fund in addition to Profit from Sales..........	11,414 59		50,049 13	
"	Sundry Creditors, on Account of Supplies.........			5,156 48	
				$55,205 61	
By	Plant, Machinery and Type..	$24,390 88			
	Less Depreciation............	3,658 62		$20,732 26	
"	Furniture and Fixtures.........	1,126 54			
	Less Depreciation............	166 58		959 96	
"	Sundry Creditors............			5,886 38	
"	Stock on Hand—				
	Books	8,668 56			
	Outfit	15,644 56			
	Engraving	500 00		24,813 12	
"	Cash at Bank.............			2,813 89	
				$55,205 61	

General Income and Expenditure Six Months Ending September 30, 1899.

NATIONAL HEADQUARTERS MAINTENANCE.

To	Rent of National Headquarters, and Officers' Quarters.	$5,301 35	$5,301 35	
"	Repairs and Alterations, Arranging New Offices, and Repairs after Fire.	3,443 44		
	Less Insurance and Rebate.	580 07	2,863 37	
"	Fuel and Light for Offices and Auditoriums, including Water Tax.	1,987 35		
"	Printing and Stationery for Headquarters General Work and Disposition of Forces.	899 80		
"	Postage, Telegrams and Telephone Service.......	1,292 97		
"	Salaries of Headquarters' Staff and Employees.......	7,945 00		
"	Legal Department. Salary, Stationery and Special Legal Service in connection with the Act of Incorporation.	2,523 54		
"	Interest on Loans, General Salvation Army Work.......	484 30		
"	Expressage and Office Ex-			
	Carried forward......	$15,132 96	$8,164 72	
By	Donations and Auxiliary Membership Subscriptions.	$2,036 96		
"	Less Departmental Expenses, Passes, Periodicals and 25 per cent. Commission to D. O's..........	860 27	$1,176 69	
"	Divisional Percentage Account. Total Receipts from Divisions.	2,732 98		
"	Less Allowance on old Accounts	400 38	$2,332 60	
"	Donations, Collections for Sick and Wounded, Homes of Rest Expenses.		1,760 44	
"	Self-Denial Fund. Total Collection received at Headquarters.............	37,293 45		
	Less Expenses of Collec-			
	Carried forward......	$37,293 45	$5,269 73	

Brought forward......	$15,132 96	$8,164 72
penses, Freight, Cartage on Furniture	765 46	
To Grants to Divisions, Corps and Officers.........	2,452 80	
" Staff and F. O. Traveling Expenses of Staff Officers to Divisional Centres, for Demonstrations, Councils of War, and General Business.	1,735 04	$20,086 26
" National Specials. Expenses of Officers set apart for Special Evangelistic Work and Corps Inspection.	1,482 53	
" Special Demonstrations. Expenses of Meetings, Printing, Postage, Traveling, Rent, &c.	1,297 70	
" Junior Soldiers' War. National Supervision, Expenses, Salaries, Traveling, &c.	1,190 89	
" Training Homes. Expenses of Homes, Maintenance, Traveling, Rents, &c.	2,048 50	
" Naval & Military League. Expenses, Stationery and Postage, including Special Operation Expenses.	291 70	
" Sick and Wounded. Homes of Rest. Expenses of Homes Maintenance of Homes, Grants.	3,393 52	9,704 84
" Social Income and Expenditure Account.	2,809 50	
" Property Department. Income and Expenditure Account .	1,942 07	4,751 57
" Balance to Salvation Army Fund.		563 30
		$43,270 69

Brought forward......	$37,293 45	$5,269 73	
tions, Printing, Advertising, Expressage, Postage, 10 per cent Commission to D. O's and one-third of Profit for Missionary Work.......		23,550 05	$18,743 40
By Transfer from Trade Department from Profit from Sales.........			24,257 56
			$43,270 69

Social and Relief Branches.

To Social Department Expenses for General Oversight, Salaries, Traveling, Stationery, Loans &c.	$3,087 63		
Less Income from Institutions for Maintenance, Expenses, Loans and Traveling returned	2,041 43	$1,046 20	
" Investigation Department. Expenses, Salaries, Stationery, Traveling, Postage, &c.	526 48		
Less Subscriptions	70 14	$456 34	
" Merchants' League. Cost of Material for Collecting purposes, Salaries, Traveling	701 70		
Less Collections	609 02	92 68	
" Expenses of Institutions for Rent, Help, Maintenance, Gas, Coal, &c—			
The Ardmore Shelter	2,711 15		
" Bowery "	2,017 40		
" Dry Dock "	1,625 91		
" Glendon "	1,573 14		
" Jersey City "	1,983 56		
" Newark "	1,777 12	$11,688 28	
" Salvage Depots, Cost of Collecting and Maintenance Expenses—			
Jersey City Salvage	930 30		
Newark	198 81	'$1,129 11	
" Slums, Rescue & Childrens' Homes—			
Slum Work	161 43		
Childrens' Home	574 20		
General Rescue Department Expenses	904 42	$1,640 05	
		$16,052 66	

By Mercy-Box Income for General Social Maintenance Expenses—			
" Receipts from Charges for Lodgings and Donations—			
The Ardmore Shelter	$2,523 35		
" Bowery "	2,374 34		
" Dry Dock "	1,703 00		
" Glendon "	1,599 63		
" Jersey City "	1,904 75		
" Newark "	1,667 70	$11,772 77	
" Receipts for Sale of Merchandise Collected—			
Jersey City Salvage	640 75		
Newark "	109 47	$750 22	
" Collections, Donations and Special Appeals—			
Slums	32 03		
Childrens' Home	395 66		
Rescue Department	292 48	$720 17	
" Balance to General Income and Expenditure Account		$2,809 50	
		$16,052 66	

Mercy Box Account.

To Mercy-Box Department, Expenses, Salary, Stationery and Postage......	$ 388 68		By Total Receipts at Head-quarters..............	$1,636 46
" Transfer to Social Department......	1,247 78	$1,636 46		
		$1,636 46		$1,636 46

Property Department.

To Interest on Mortgages......	$ 819 12	$6,284 92	By Rents of Properties, Halls, for Interest......	$6,013 57	
" Repairs to Properties......			" Donation of Property for Salvation Army Purposes..	2,475 00	
" Departmental Expenses, including Depreciation in Real Estate through Sales of Disused Properties......	3,200 98		" General Income and Expenditure......	1,942 07	$10,430 64
" Insurance on Buildings and Properties	125 62	$4,145 72			
		$10,430 64			$10,430 64

Funeral Fund.

To Expenses of Funerals and Plots... Sick and Wounded	$ 720 89		By Balance from March 31st, 1899......	$ 901 02	
" Grant to Sick and Wounded Fund......	1,500 00		" Income and Transfer from Divisional Indebtedness...	2,279 77	$3,180 79
		2,220 89			
		959 90			
" Balance carried down......		$3,180 79			
		$3,180 79			$3,180 79

Disabled Officers' Fund.

To Grants to Disabled Officers during Six Months......	$ 1,136 85		By Balance, March 31st, 1899	$10,968 88	
" Balance brought down.....	10,815 89	$11,952 74	" Commission from War Cry Sales	983 86	$11,952 74
		$11,952 74			$11,952 74

Balance Sheet for Six Months Ending September 30, 1899.

To Loans on Mortgages, reported March 31st, 1899, on Lease and Freehold Properties..	$291,454 75			
" Mortgages added during half year on Farm Colonies and additional Properties secured	66,541 45	$357,996 20		
" Sundry Creditors, Corps for Building purposes...		5,221 70		
" Sundry Creditors. Loans and Trust Money, secured by Notes and Mortgages, Relief, Disabled Officers, Funeral, Collection, Armenian, Special and Legacy..		15,743 34		
" Sundry International Accounts for Missionary Work, Loans, &c...		11,489 47		
"Sundry Creditors, Loans for fixed periods...		28,625 15		
" Sundry Creditors for Colonization Purposes...		46,455 06		
" Salvation Army Fund, March 31st, 1899	318,740 92			
" Income and Expenditure Account ...	563 30	319,304 22		
		$784,835 14		
By Freehold and Leasehold Property reported March 31st, 1899.........		$607,856 82		
Additions during six months, Colonies and other Property		63,738 89		
Less Depreciation..........		671,595 71		
		2,066 00	669,529 71	
" Furniture and Fixtures, National Headquarters......		12,000 00		
Addition during six months		2,571 12	14,571 12	
" Sundry Debtors, Loans on Properties			2,434 45	
" Sundry Debtors, Loans to Divisions, Corps and Sundry Salvation Army operations			27,939 29	
" Colonies for Improvement on Lands, Houses and Instalments.			58,476 66	
" Social Furniture and Fixtures, March 1899		10,792 44		
Addition during six months		291 65	11,084 19	
" Cash at Bank.........			799 72	
			$784,835 14	

Trade Department.

BALANCE SHEET FOR HALF YEAR ENDING SEPTEMBER 30, 1899.

To Stock reported April 1st, 1899	$50,049 13			
" Profit and Loss, after deducting Grant to General Fund	517 85	$50,566 98		
" Sundry Creditors on account of Supplies...		7,015 15		
		$57,582 13		
By Plant, Machinery, as reported March 31st, 1899..	$20,732 26			
Additions during six months	2,081 81	$22,814 07		
" Furniture and Fixtures....		959 96		
" Sundry Debtors..........		15,375 36		
" Stock on Hand—				
Book	6,000 00			
Outfit	8,000 00			
Engraving	500 00	14,500 00		
" Cash on Hand..		3,982 74		
		$57,582 13		

STATE OF NEW YORK.
CITY AND COUNTY OF NEW YORK. } ss.

On this 16th day of December, 1899, before me personally appeared, J. E. Bliss, Jr., who being by me duly sworn, did depose and say that he is an expert accountant and public auditor. That as such an accountant and auditor he has examined in detail the books of The Salvation Army Incorporated; that he has verified the footings in said books, and finds a voucher for expenditure of money; and he finds all the entries, footings and postings to be true and correct; that the foregoing is a true and correct abstract and balance sheet from the said books.

J. E. Bliss, Jr.

Subscribed and sworn to before me this 16th day of December, 1899.

M. J. H. Ferris,
Notary Public,
New York City.

[SEAL.]

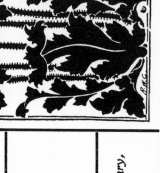

THE *Trade Catalogue* contains a complete list of the Books, Pens, Texts, Teas, Uniforms, Stereopticons and other goods sold by The Salvation Army through their Central Trade Depot, in New York.

For particulars write to Brigadier Caygill, Trade Secretary, 120 West Fourteenth Street, New York City.

Salvation Army Bibliography.

BY GENERAL WILLIAM BOOTH
(Founder of The Salvation Army.)

In Darkest England and the Way Out $0 75
The Training of Children, cloth, red edges 1 00
General Booth's Letters $0 75
The Why and Wherefore of The Salvation Army 0 25

BY THE LATE MRS CATHERINE BOOTH
(Mother of The Salvation Army.)

Practical Religion $0 75
Popular Christianity 75
Aggressive Christianity 75
Life and Death $0 55
Godliness 75
The Salvation Army in relation to Church and State 25

BY COMMANDER BOOTH TUCKER.

The Life of Catherine Booth, being a history of The Salvation
Army and the early lives of its founders. Two vols., 8vo.,
cloth $3 50
A Short Life of William Booth, General of The Salvation Army. $0 05
$3.00 per hundred.

Short Tracts on the Problem of the Poor :

The Farm Colonies of The Salvation Army $0 05
Our Future Pauper Policy 05
Back to the Land 03
The Salvation Army in the United States being a pictorial report
of the work, profusely illustrated and including last annual
balance sheet $0 05

BY COMMISSIONER RAILTON.

Twenty-one Years' Salvation Army, a sketch of the early days of
the Army $0 75
All About The Salvation Army, by those who know $0 05

COMPILED BY COMMANDER BOOTH TUCKER.

One Hundred Favorite Songs of The Salvation Army, being the music and words of 100 of the Army's most popular songs by General Booth, Commander and Consul Booth Tucker, Major Slater and others, and including several melodies by Professor Chas. K. Harris and Paul Dresser, with Army words, such as "Just Break the News to Mother," "The Banks of the Wabash," "After the Ball," and "Just Tell Her that You Saw Me," also the words of 50 other songs and 300 choruses
Boards .... $0 25 | Cloth $0 05
Song Book containing the words only of all the above. $0 50

Periodicals.

"War Cry," published weekly in New York, being the official
gazette of The Salvation Army in the United States. Yearly
subscription, post paid $2 00
"Pacific Coast War Cry," published in San Francisco. 2 00
"Stridsropet" published weekly in New York, being the Scandinavian-American edition of the "War Cry," 1 25
"Der Kriegsruf," published fortnightly in New York, being the
German-American edition of the "War Cry",.... .... 0 70
"Chinese War Cry," published occasionally in San Francisco,
per copy.......... .... $0 05
"Young Soldier," published weekly in New York, being the
children's edition of the "War Cry," 0 50
"Harbor Lights," published monthly in New York, being specially intended to represent the Army in the United States
and in other lands for the information of Auxiliaries and
friends.... .... 0 50

DEPARTMENT OF SOCIAL ECONOMY

FOR THE

UNITED STATES COMMISSION TO THE PARIS EXPOSITION OF 1900

MONOGRAPHS

ON

AMERICAN SOCIAL ECONOMICS

EDITOR

HERBERT B. ADAMS

Professor of American History in Johns Hopkins University

ASSOCIATE EDITOR

RICHARD WATERMAN JR

XX

The Social Relief Work of the Salvation Army in the United States

BY

COMMANDER BOOTH TUCKER

THIS MONOGRAPH IS CONTRIBUTED TO THE UNITED STATES SOCIAL ECONOMY EXHIBIT BY THE LEAGUE FOR SOCIAL SERVICE, NEW YORK

J. B. LYON COMPANY
PRINTERS AND BINDERS
ALBANY, N. Y.

TABLE OF CONTENTS

SOCIAL RELIEF WORK OF THE SALVATION ARMY IN THE UNITED STATES:

GENERAL WILLIAM BOOTH

FOUNDER OF THE SALVATION ARMY

COMMANDER AND CONSUL BOOTH TUCKER, IN CHARGE OF THE SALVATION ARMY WORK
IN THE UNITED STATES

SOCIAL RELIEF WORK OF THE SALVATION ARMY IN THE UNITED STATES

CHAPTER I.

GENESIS OF THE SALVATION ARMY

The mudpools of society possess a peculiar interest for the sociologist, be he humanitarian or statesman. Hunger amounting to positive starvation, destitution that means the actual lack of the most common necessaries of existence, misery that represents a Niagara of tears, intertangled with a ghastly profusion of blasphemy, vermin, vice and crime, constitute a dark background to what would indeed be a loathsome picture, but for the fact that it is illumined with lightning flashes of love, piety and patient endurance, whose existence might least be suspected amid such sad surroundings. Here the dividing line between earth and hell becomes so hard to locate that those who inhabit this sombre shadowland of woe ofttimes feel and seem as though they had already passed from the one to the other.

Into this desolate region the Salvation army flung itself, nay from its very vortex of misery it may be said to have originated. The international developments and multitudinous outgrowths of the movement were represented at its inception by two solitary individuals, whom Providence had first linked together, and then plunged into the midst of this maelstrom of sin and sorrow. Singlehanded, unsupported by material resources of any kind, William and Catherine Booth planted the standard of salvation as near the gates of hell as they could reach.

It was in July, 1865, on Mile End Waste, in the east end of London, amid vice, degradation and squalor probably without parallel in any corner of the globe, that they commenced their work of spiritual and social reform.

3

They adapted their methods to the savage hordes of semi-barbarians to whom they had consecrated their lives. Their first citadels were planted in the heart of sindom and slumdom. Over the doorway of one of these was written the strange inscription: "No respectable people admitted." The sinners they were after gloried in their savagery. Their Bible was the "penny dreadful," their place of worship the saloon, their god their unbridled appetites, their prayer hideous blasphemy. No church-door was ever darkened with their shadow. They were neither expected, nor wanted. The sight of their unkempt condition would have driven away the usual worshippers.

But the dime museums and "penny gaffs," which these misfits of humanity had been accustomed to frequent, were pressed into service by this Prophet of the poor. They were quickly crowded to the doors with the rowdy element he sought to reach. Amongst the earliest converts were prize-fighters, pigeon-flyers, gamblers, drunkards, criminals, many of them notorious for their wickedness.

Each captured gun was turned against the enemy. Each prisoner of war was drilled as a recruit. His simple testimony became a powerful weapon of offense. Multitudes who would not cross the road to hear a preacher, crowded to hear the broken sentences of the champion wrestler, or lightweight boxer who had been their hero. Here they could listen to the simple vernacular to which they were themselves accustomed. The very breakdowns of the speakers were more interesting than the polished flights of the most eloquent orator. Their arguments were resistless. What they recommended they possessed. What they had gained was surely within each listener's reach, since their circumstances and surroundings were the same.

The powerful influence of woman's ministry was also introduced, and helped to sway the savage throng. Riots were quelled and bloodshed prevented by those fearless, calm-eyed women, often mere girls, who dared to cast themselves into this lion's den of humanity.

NATIONAL HEADQUARTERS FOR AMERICA, 120-124 WEST 14TH ST., NEW YORK

Even the music and singing were revolutionized for the purposes of this modern crusade. The popular tap-room melodies of the day were fitted to suitable words, so simple that a child could understand,— often mere doggerel, it was true, and not always either rhythmical or grammatical. If they conveyed their meaning, that was the great point. Would the tune " go? " If not, however beautiful it might be, it was ruthlessly discarded as unsuited for the great end in view.

Military methods and titles were not added till the year 1879. They undoubtedly served to lend speed and strength to the movement.

The work was commenced on purely spiritual lines. The founder, William Booth, had already attained national fame as a revivalist. Not a little of his inspiration had been drawn from the two great American evangelists, Caughey and Finney. The passionate fervor of the one, the logical precision of the other, may be traced in much of the army teachings and operations. Indeed it may be said that America was represented at the very cradle of the Salvation army.

It is not to be wondered therefore that the Salvation army had scarcely become firmly established in England, when its operations were extended to America. One of its early converts settled in Cleveland, Ohio, in 1872, and immediately commenced work. After his departure nothing further was done till 1880, when another convert settled in Philadelphia. In the following year, in answer to an urgent appeal, reinforcements were dispatched under Commissioner George S. Railton, and from that moment the work went forward apace.

The present operations of the Salvation army in the United States embrace the following particulars:

Seven hundred corps and outposts; 2600 officers and employees; 160 social relief institutions for the poor; 450 officers and employees in charge of same; 7000 accommodation provided by social institutions; 11,000 open-air and indoor meetings held weekly; 2,200,000 average number of persons attending meetings weekly; 20,000 unpaid workers mostly wearing uniform; 50,000 average number of yearly conversions; 52 shelters for men and women; 5000 accommodation in same; 23 cheap food depots; 19 salvage brigades and workshops for the unemployed; 222 accommodation in same; 51 officers and employees in charge; 17 trades and industries; 8 labor bureaus; 3 farm colonies; 1800 acres of land; 200 colonists, including men, women and children; 20 slum posts; 41 slum officers; 14 rescue homes for fallen women; 360 accommodation in same; 1000 girls permanently or temporarily helped; 2 children's homes for waifs and strays; 66 accommodation in same.

CHAPTER 2

SOCIAL SALVATION

As its name signifies, the Salvation army was originally started with the sole aim of reaching the non-church-going masses with the Gospel. Here was the appalling statement made by those who had given the matter years of patient study, that 90% of the working classes in the older civilizations of Europe habitually neglected public worship and had practically cut themselves loose from even the outward profession of religion. It was to remedy this condition of affairs that William and Catherine Booth set to work.

As evangelists they could crowd the largest buildings with the vast crowds who flocked to their meetings. Their converts were numbered by thousands. Yet they could not fail to notice and mourn over the fact that those who came were mostly church-goers and professors of religion. The godless multitudes drifted past their doors. To reach them, other methods must be pursued. Their habits must be studied and they must be followed to their haunts and hiding-places.

When, however, this had been done, it became daily more and more evident that the evils to be combatted were of a

SALVATION ARMY DIVISIONAL HEADQUARTERS FOR NEW ENGLAND AND CENTRAL WORKINGMEN'S HOTEL, BOSTON, MASS.

temporal as well as of a spiritual character. Churchlessness was with these classes the natural outcome of homelessness, worklessness and worthlessness. To combat the evil, its causes must be radically dealt with. The task was truly a gigantic one. But General Booth was not the man to shrink from it. Cautiously and experimentally at first, and finally with the confidence that was the natural outcome of repeated success, he grappled with the problem.

In traversing and transforming these melancholy wastes of woe, root principles were discovered and laid down for the guidance of the legion of well-trained workers who had been rapidly enrolled.

The poor were to be treated with love, and not with suspicion or contempt.

They were to be classified, not as the worthy and unworthy, but as those who were willing to work out their own regeneration, and the unwilling.

They were to be encouraged in every possible way to become their own deliverers.

Each institution was to aim at self-support by the labor or payments of its inmates.

Social reform to be complete must include the soul as well as the body. In other words the man himself must be changed and not merely his circumstances.

To save a man for this world should be but a stepping-stone toward saving him for the next.

Finally, in the fall of 1890, the outcome of the previous year's experiments was tabulated and published by General Booth in a book which quickly received world-wide recognition. The publication of *In darkest England and the way out* undoubtedly marked a new era in the history of sociology. The problems which were discussed in those pages with masterly ability were quickly recognized as belonging to the world rather than to any single country, and the remedies suggested commended themselves to the ablest students of the question.

In England a fund of $600,000 was subscribed in the course of a few days to enable General Booth to put his plans into operation on a larger scale. That the confidence thus manifested toward him was not misplaced has been universally acknowledged and is proven by the following statistics, showing the vast scale upon which those operations are now being conducted throughout the world. The figures given are for the 12 months ending June 30, 1899. It would be safe to add at least 20% to these figures on account of recently opened institutions for which returns were not complete:

One hundred and fifty-eight food depots and shelters for men and women; 13,533 sleeping accommodation in same; 3,697,860 beds supplied during year; 5,968,365 meals supplied during year; 60 workshops and salvage brigades for temporary employment of out-of-works; 48,512 persons supplied with work in same; 37 labor bureaus; 6367 persons found situations; 17 children's homes and day nurseries; 23,245 children sheltered; 11 farm colonies; 5562 acres of land occupied; 450 colonists, including men, women and children; 121 slum posts; 464,113 hours spent in slum visitation; 11 homes for ex-criminals; 382 accommodation in same; 1626 ex-criminals passed through during year; 1393 satisfactory cases; 91 rescue homes for fallen women; 1894 accommodation in same; 5132 girls passed through during year; 3449 satisfactory cases; 1604 missing persons found during year; 39 other social institutions; 545 total social institutions; 2062 officers and employees in charge of same.

CHAPTER 3

THE PROBLEM OF POVERTY IN AMERICA

Pauperdom has undoubtedly not attained the same proportions in America as in the older civilizations of Europe. Probably the percentage in the former is not more than five, whereas in the latter it is estimated at 10.

The census of 1890 shows that the inmates of public and private institutions for paupers and criminals numbered no less than 340,000, while at least 10 times that number pass through these institutions during the year. It is fair, therefore, to estimate the numbers of those who live on the borders of pauperdom in the United States at not less than 3,000,000 souls.

This estimate is confirmed by the fact that during the exceptionally prosperous conditions now existing the returns of the various labor unions in the state of New York show that 10% of their members are out of work. For the previous quarter the average was 18%, and in ordinary seasons, apart from any unusual depression, the percentage is considerably higher.

It is fair to suppose that the condition of the wage-earners who are members of unions is an index of the condition of nonunion labor, the probability being that there is a larger proportion of out-of-works among the latter than the former.

From the above facts it may be regarded as certain that the "submerged" classes in America, including the criminal, the vicious and the purely pauper elements, number not less than 3,000,000 under favorable sociological circumstances, while the number is liable to increase alarmingly during seasons of commercial depression.

For dealing with this mass of poverty and suffering the Salvation army in the United States has organized the various institutions and agencies described in the following pages. These include:

Shelters for homeless men; shelters for homeless women; homes for clerks and artisans; homes for girls working in stores and offices; homes for children; rescue homes for fallen women; slum posts for slum visitation and meetings; slum day nurseries for infants; cheap food depots and cent-meals; cheap clothing and second-hand stores; salvage brigades for collection of household and office waste; woodyards; employment bureaus; Knights of hope for prison visitation and ex-criminals; winter relief; medical relief, including free hospital and dispensaries; summer outings for the poor; penny ice wagons; Christmas and Thanksgiving dinners; missing friends and inquiry department; farm colonies for the poor.

The complex character of the remedies above indicated has been necessitated by the complex nature of the evil to be dealt with. To the uninitiated eye poverty appears to be one seething cauldron of dirt, rags, hunger, hypocrisy and misery. To the skilled eye of our officers, who devote their lives to the practical task of combatting the evil, the poor may be divided into classes which are as sharply defined and unmixable as the castes of the Hindoos, or the stratas of geology. To deal successfully with the monster of poverty, each of its hydra heads must be separately handled, with methods peculiar to itself and with a staff of workers who are trained to become experts in their own particular department, whilst the sunshine of love and the tender showers of Gospel grace are made to permeate the mass.

CHAPTER 4

SHELTERS FOR HOMELESS MEN

Every large city in America has its quota of homeless men. Their home, if such it can be called, is the low lodging-house. As a rule the accommodation is of the meanest character. The rooms and bedding abound with vermin, making sleep well-nigh impossible.

Let me describe a night spent in one of these dens in New York. The building was a tall brick structure, with accommodation for perhaps 300 men. As I passed across a kind of gangway, my guide, who was one of our slum soldiers, informed me that more than one murder had been committed on that dark spot, the victims being flung into a sort of cellar below. We were directed to a large room, the only furniture

SALVATION ARMY WORKINGMEN'S HOTEL, PHILADELPHIA

of which consisted of a large stove and about 50 canvas hammocks, slung in double-decker fashion from a couple of bars that ran the length of the room. All the lower hammocks being occupied, I had to content myself with an upper. It was a bitterly cold night, but the fire was out, and there was no bedding. The cold alone made sleep impossible. The one rough article of clothing which I took off formed my pillow. Beneath it I placed my shoes, which would otherwise probably have been missing by daylight. The hacking coughs of many of the men showed that hardship and exposure were rapidly doing their work. In spite of the vermin, the cold and the noises I dozed off for a few moments. Whether I dreamed or snored I can not say, but I woke up in time to hear the man who was sleeping under me say to another who was wandering about the room, perhaps seeing what he could pick up, "There's a bum in that doss!" "Stick a pin into him!" responded the other. "Go and fetch the boss," remarked some one else. The speakers evidently had no idea that the "bum" in the "doss" was the commander of the Salvation army, personally investigating the condition of the working classes, and the sort of accommodation afforded them in an average lodging-house in New York!

Since that day we have opened in and around New York six workingmen's shelters, accommodating 736 homeless men. An iron spring bed with mattrass, pillow, sheets and blankets can be obtained for 10 cents, while those who prefer a room to themselves can obtain one for an additional nickel. Each dormitory is warmed with a stove, while hot and cold baths, wash-tubs and a reading-room are provided free of charge. The officer in command takes a kindly interest in the men, gets to know each of them individually and helps to find them employment when out of work.

Similar institutions have been provided in the following cities: Chicago, Boston, Philadelphia, Cleveland, Toledo, Pittsburg, Providence, Buffalo, Rochester, Syracuse, Fall

River, Waterbury, Cincinnati, Louisville, Nashville, St Louis, Springfield, Ill., Little Rock, Kansas City, Denver, Cripple Creek, Salt Lake City, Portland, Ore., and San Francisco. In some of the largest of these cities from two to five shelters have been opened, and there appears no end to the possibilities of developing this class of work.

To remove these men from the contaminating surroundings of the moral cesspools which they are otherwise compelled to frequent, and to encircle them with healthy, holy influences, is a work the importance of which it is impossible to exaggerate. We have now 45 shelters for homeless men in the United States, with accommodation for 5000 persons.

CHAPTER 5

SHELTERS FOR HOMELESS WOMEN

Happily the number of homeless women is far less than that of homeless men. Nevertheless most large cities possess a considerable and alas increasing class of those whose relations have died, or deserted them, and who pick up a scanty subsistence by charring, cleaning offices and doing odd jobs, or selling cheap wares in the streets. They are less migratory than the men, and soon make our shelters their permanent " home."

Some of them have been addicted to liquor. "We can always get a drink for nothing from some friendly saloon-keeper by doing some odd job for him, such as cleaning the windows, when we can not get either money or food," said one of these women apologetically to the shelter officer, who had charged her with drinking. " It stops the cravings of hunger," she added.

The warmth, the light, the cleanliness of our shelters, and above all the kindness with which they are treated, serve to work a speedy reformation. "Some of them," said a shelter officer, " exhibit symptoms of hydrophobia at the very sight

SALVATION HOTEL FOR YOUNG WOMEN EMPLOYED IN STORES

of water, when they first come to us.   But they soon get to
appreciate the value of cleanliness, and many of them give
their hearts to God.   Saddest of all is, when we have to turn
some away, because every bed is occupied.   Oh how they
plead with us just to let them sleep on the floor, or in the
passages."

Our New York shelter was commenced in a building just
off Chatham Square.   Our license allowed only 44 beds.
These were soon regularly occupied, and we took a larger
building in the heart of the Bowery, with accommodation for
100.   During the summer months the attendance has steadily
increased so that the beds are now all occupied, and numbers
have to be turned away.   A second building has already become necessary.

In Chicago and San Francisco similar shelters have been
opened, although on a smaller scale, with similar results.

Perhaps no sight is sadder than that of these homeless and
friendless women, struggling bravely to earn the pittance which
shall enable them to keep out of the dreaded poorhouse.   The
census states that 74,521 of the women in the national public
and private institutions for the poor assign as the cause of
their dependence the "want of another home," while 94%
of them are stated to be "able-bodied," capable, that is,
of some moderate amount of work.   In the majority of
cases they are not even to be blamed for their condition.
The death of the bread-winner, abandonment, or misfortune
have, in most cases, brought them to the border land of destitution.   And yet they struggle bravely on, glad and thankful if they can only be independent of society's aid, with no
hope of the honored rest their silvered hair and stoop of age
might claim.

Tenderly our officers minister to their spiritual, as well as
temporal needs, and the joy of a future "home" and "rest"
for their soul palliates the toil and loneliness of their present lot.

CHAPTER 6

HOMES FOR ARTISANS

In several cities homes have been opened, where clerks, storesmen and others of the artisan classes can get accommodation a little superior to that provided in our ordinary shelters, and yet for a very small outlay. This has been greatly appreciated, and has helped to constitute a step upwards for many of those whom our cheaper institutions have rescued from the lowest depths of suffering, besides acting as a valuable prevention for numbers who were in danger of lapsing into the same condition.

In many of our large shelters a separate floor with superior accommodation at a slightly increased charge is set apart for this purpose, thus avoiding the expense of renting an extra building and requiring an additional staff.

It is found preferable, however, where there is a sufficient demand, to have an entirely separate building. This has already been done, with excellent effect in Boston and Kansas City.

These moral safeguards from the pernicious influences which drag down so many of our young men may well be multiplied.

CHAPTER 7

HOMES FOR WORKING GIRLS

In all the large cities of the United States thousands of young women are employed in the stores and offices. While many of those have happily homes of their own, a vast proportion are obliged to board out. The inducements to vice are terrible. To pay for rent and food out of the $4 to $6 a week which their wages average, besides dressing with the neatness which their employers demand, is well-nigh impossible. To starve or sell their virtue becomes the painful alternative. At least the gateway of vice is dangerously near and

SALVATION ARMY ORPHANAGE, SAN FRANCISCO

wide open to those young and inexperienced feet. To help them after they have fallen is good,— to prevent their fall is infinitely better.

A painful story is told of a young girl in one of our cities applying vainly for admission at the door of the various institutions. She could not be received because she had not fallen. Driven to despair, she returned soon afterwards saying, " Now I have done what you wanted. Now I am truly fallen and I have a right to claim admission."

There can be no doubt that cheap homes for respectable young women are daily becoming a greater necessity in our cities. We have already established several such.

Our home in Boston has been named after the late Washington Benedict, who was deeply interested in the establishment of such an institution. Our Flower home in Los Angeles was presented to the Salvation army by the ladies' committee, who had been managing it for several years. The property is valued at $20,000, and is beautifully situated in the center of the city. The officer in charge holds a medical diploma.

CHAPTER 8

CHILDREN'S HOMES

" Damned into the world rather than born into it," some one has said, are the children of our slums. The tenements of our great cities swarm with those who answer to this pitiful description. Cradled from their infancy in disease, misery, vice and crime, little wonder that many of them grow up to be the terrors of the society that has so often neglected them.

Often the only fault of the parents is their poverty. "It is only that I am hungry, but mother says I must not tell!" said a little boy, who had fainted away in one of our meetings. And then the sad story leaked out. His father, an honest working man, had been out of employment for weeks. In vain had he walked the streets day after day in search of work. For some time the mother had painfully battled with the wolf at the door by means of needle-work. Finally she had broken down beneath the strain. She was ill in bed, and the seven children were literally starving. There was no food in the attic which served as home. Help was quickly sent, the father was found work, and before long the whole family was comfortably established in a little home. It was a cold Christmas and the snow was on the ground. Little Freddy ran to the window, threw it open and flung out a handful of crumbs for the birds. " See, mama," he cried glee-fully, "last Christmas we had no crumbs for ourselves. This Christmas we have plenty for the birds as well."

Our New York and San Francisco homes for orphans and destitute children accommodate about 60 such, and every available bed is occupied, while we are reluctantly compelled to refuse many a little needy lamb, it being impossible to make this branch of our operations self-supporting, as we are able to do with most of the others.

It is intended at an early date to establish a branch home on one of our farm colonies, with a special view to teaching the children agricultural pursuits and finally planting them out in homes of their own. This seems preferable to the ex-isting plan of placing them out in the iamilles of farmers, as under our system they will become homeowners and not merely farm laborers.

CHAPTER 9

RESCUE HOMES FOR FALLEN WOMEN

It is estimated that in the United States alone no less than 50,000 girls annually pass from the ranks of the fallen to a premature grave. Their places, alas, are quickly taken by others, so that there is no apparent diminution in the volume of vice which pours its Niagara of woe through our streets and homes.

More sinned against than sinning, the doors of society are closed tightly against these human derelicts, the wreckage and wreckers of our homes and youth.

WORK ROOM IN THE SALVATION ARMY RESCUE HOME, NEW YORK

To deal with them successfully it has been found necessary to organize an entirely different set of institutions, or rather homes, under the supervision of a staff of officers who are trained wholly and solely for this class of work, and who thus acquire an experience and achieve a success which would not otherwise be possible.

Fourteen homes with accommodation for 360 girls have been established in the following cities of the United States: New York, Boston, Chicago, St Louis, Philadelphia, Cleveland, Buffalo, Grand Rapids, St Paul, Omaha, Des Moines, Portland, Los Angeles and San Francisco.

Including preventive cases and those who have only stayed a few days, about 1000 girls have passed through these homes during the past year. The percentage of satisfactory cases is more than 80%.

We aim at keeping the girls about four months in the home. They help to meet their expenses by various kinds of needle-work, such as the making of texts, uniforms and garments, as well as by bookbinding, chicken-raising and other occupations. The majority of them are trained for housework and sent out to suitable situations. The value of work done in the homes during the last 12 months amounted to nearly $3000.

At the time of writing, 60 babies are being cared for in the homes, indeed the maternity department of this work is assuming increasing importance.

A volume could easily be filled with the sad stories of betrayal, of cruelty and crime, which are poured into the ears of our officers by these unhappy victims of vice. But a single instance must suffice.

It was a cold miserable evening in winter. A woman stood on the banks of the Mississippi, her babe wrapped in her arms. She had made up her mind to bury her sorrows in the waters of the river. Home and friends had closed their doors against her. The one for whose sake she had risked all had deserted

her. Death itself seemed preferable to such an existence as
had fallen to her lot.

Just then a drum-beat, followed by music and singing, fell
upon her ear. It was the nightly march and open-air of the
Salvation army. Nearer and nearer they drew. Not far
from the spot where the would-be suicide was standing they
halted, formed a ring and commenced their service. The quick
eye of the girl-captain read the despair that was imprinted on
that fair young face. A few kind words of sympathy drew her
to the hall, and before the meeting closed, the story of sorrow
and shame had been whispered into the captain's ear, and salvation sought at the cross.

One of our rescue homes quickly opened its doors to receive
the Magdalene and her babe, and then in due course a position of usefulness was found, with an opportunity to start the
voyage of life under new and happier auspices. Some years
later the incident was related in a public meeting. A well-
dressed woman rose and asked permission to speak. "The
story you have heard is all true," she said. "I am the woman
referred to. I have now a happy home and a good husband,
and can not express my gratitude to the army for having saved
me from a suicide's grave and brought me to a knowledge of
salvation."

CHAPTER 10

SLUM WORK

Who has not heard of "Hell's Kitchen," "The Bowery,"
"The Tenderloin," or "Cherry street?" The very names
have become world-famous, as synonyms for debauchery,
slumdom and crime. In the very heart of these citadels of
sin the Salvation army has planted its outposts. The girl-
warriors who have dared to storm these "forts of darkness"
have done so in the first instance at the risk of their lives.
Pelted with refuse, treated with ignominy, threatened with
violence, they have persisted in their noble work, till a permanent footing has been gained.

Now, how different is their position. They are known by the name of " slum angels." At any hour of the day or night they can walk down streets or alleys where the police will only pass in twos. If a fight is going on, they will make straight for the center of the crowd, as the recognized peacemakers of the poor, and woe betide the man who lays a finger upon them. The worst dives and saloons are open to their ministrations.

" There are only two saloons," says the officer in charge of our Chicago slumwork, " where our girls are not admitted, and these two are visited by them regularly every week. When the boss says, ' Did I not tell you not to come here any more? ' the captain replies, ' Yes, sir! But I have come to see whether you have changed your mind! ' "

In the city of Cleveland one of the most notorious saloon-keepers and criminals was converted and has stood faithful for some years past. When his saloon was first visited by our women officers, he poured a schooner of beer down their backs as they knelt to pray! This man was popularly known as " The Ferret." His picture hangs in the Rogues' gallery of the United States, but the face has been turned to the wall, since the police are well aware that Fred Ford is converted and is earning an honest living.

Our slum officers live in the heart of slumdom, and minister day and night to the sick and suffering. In order to make themselves more one with the people they have adopted an even simpler and humbler garb than that worn by our ordinary officers. A poke bonnet would appear too respectable, and even extravagant, to those whose lives are spent in one long desperate struggle with poverty.

In New York alone we have 20 slum officers entirely set apart for work of this character, while other slum posts have been opened in Boston, Chicago, Philadelphia, Providence, Cincinnati, Cleveland and St Louis.

Not the least important feature of the slum officer's work

is her nightly meeting. Gathered together in her hall is an intensely interesting collection of the toughest characters in the city. With wonderful skill and patience she handles them. Strange to say, although the meetings are of a strictly religious character, they possess for these wastrels of society a peculiar fascination. The greatest punishment that can be inflicted for a serious breach of discipline is exclusion from the meetings for a time. To see the girl captain march off a disturber of the peace, maintain order and go on with the meeting, as if nothing particular had happened, is in itself a marvel of spiritual conquest and control.

These Jeanne d'Arcs of the slums are filled with a sense of their divine mission and are accepted by their rough hearers as the modern apostles of "Poverty Row."

CHAPTER II

SLUM CRECHE OR DAY NURSERY

It was found by our slum officers in the course of their visitations that in many families where the mother was the breadwinner, she would go forth in the morning, locking the door on her babe, till she returned home in the evening. What else could she do? It was impossible for her to take baby with her to her work.

Hence a slum creche soon became a necessary adjunct to this portion of our work. The mother brings her baby in the morning, leaves it for the day, and fetches it away in the evening. Wonderful reformations have thus been wrought in the way of cleanliness and health, as well as moral surroundings.

The little ones learn to sing the army songs and carry back to their miserable garrets an atmosphere of joy and brightness which has hitherto been unknown. A small charge of five cents is made to cover the cost of milk and food.

Occasionally the mother, who called in the morning, appears no more to claim the child, and then it becomes necessary to find some permanent home. But kind friends seldom fail to return a ready response to our appeal.

CHAPTER 12

CHEAP FOOD DEPOTS AND CENT MEALS

The provision of cheap, wholesome food for the poor at prices within their reach has become one of the most important branches of our work. In a single month 110,584 meals were furnished, being at the rate of more than 1,300,000 per year.

In some cases "cent meals" have been established with a special view of reaching the poor in their homes. For one cent a pint of coffee with a chunk of bread, or if preferred, a basin of soup, will be furnished. This can either be taken home or eaten on the premises.

Thus help and hope are brought to the doors of many who are too proud to make their wants known even to their dearest friends. It is by such that the pinch of poverty is the most severely felt, and it is they who are the most deserving of help, being so eager to do all in their power to help themselves.

It is sad to admit that with our advanced civilization multitudes should suffer from the actual gnawings of hunger, and yet such is undoubtedly the case. An old woman was found ill in her garret. For days she had not tasted food. She had struggled bravely on, supporting herself and her granddaughter, till sickness had laid her aside. Yet there was no spirit of complaint. Grateful for the help that had been brought. she explained to the officer who was caring for her that she had discovered a splendid remedy for the pangs of hunger when she had no food, and that was to drink hot water with a pinch of salt. "Have you ever tried it?" she asked. "You will find it wonderful for taking away the craving."

Not long ago it was stated by the teachers of the New York public schools that the children frequently came breakfastless to their lessons and that the only luncheon many of them brought was a paltry sandwich, consisting of two thin slices of bread, with some vegetable or cheese sliced between. And yet, so sensitive were the children about accepting anything that savored of "charity," that they would refuse food when it was proffered to them free of charge. It was only by inviting one and another to share their meal as a special treat, that the teacher could prevail on them to accept anything beyond the scanty meal they brought.

CHAPTER 13

CHEAP CLOTHING AND SECOND-HAND STORES

Next to the need for food and shelter comes that for clothing during our inclement winter. To provide for this, "junk shops" have been opened in some of our large cities, where second-hand articles of clothing can be bought by the poor for nominal sums. Our store in Chicago employs seven persons. Shoes are repaired, articles of clothing mended and furniture renewed, and then sold at prices which bring them within reach of all.

During the terrible blizzard of 1899 when trains were blocked and traffic obstructed the suffering among the poor was most acute. A woman came to our headquarters through the snow which was piled several feet high in the streets. A babe was in her arms, but a few weeks old, wrapped in a piece of China cloth. Her own garments were scarcely better. She was gladly supplied with what she needed. "Do not think me ungrateful," she said, when rising to leave, "if I ask you to find me one thing more. Could you let me have a pair of old shoes?" It was then that the fact was discovered that she had nothing but a little brown paper which she had placed between her stockings and the soles of her shoeless feet to protect her during that terrible tramp through the snow. Her gratitude was unbounded when this need also had been met.

CHAPTER 14

SALVAGE BRIGADES FOR THE COLLECTION OF WASTE

The urgent necessity of finding temporary employment for the out-of-works led to the conception of the collection of household and office waste. The fact that those who needed help came from so many different trades, and that it would have required a vast amount of capital to employ each in what he might happen to know, made it necessary to look out for plans which would be suitable for all sorts of labor, whether skilled or unskilled.

To collect and sell waste paper, clothing, shoes, old furniture, packing cases, bottles and articles of a similar character has been found to supply a maximum of work at a minimum of cost. The income from the sale of such goods has been usually sufficient to almost cover working expenses, the chief difficulty being to obtain the capital necessary to purchase teams, and fit up suitable buildings.

The most extensive and successful salvage brigade hitherto established is in the city of Chicago, where we have taken a contract for keeping the streets in several wards free from waste paper. Some 25 tons of waste paper are weekly handled by the brigade.

In the city of Boston 500 baskets have been placed in the houses of citizens. These are periodically cleared, and the contents disposed of through our junk store.

Salvage brigades have also been established in Brooklyn, Jersey City and Newark.

CHAPTER 15

WOODYARDS

In some cities woodyards have been started for the temporary employment of out-of-works. The necessity of finding capital for the purchase of lumber, and the difficulty of competing with machine-cut wood, has prevented us from extending this class of work on the scale that we should desire. It is, however, one of the best and simplest plans for utilizing waste labor during periods of temporay depression.

Our principal woodyards are in Waterbury, Boston, Houston, San Francisco and Seattle.

CHAPTER 16
EMPLOYMENT BUREAU

The lamentable fact that employment agencies have been so largely used by unprincipled persons for decoying the poor and fleecing them of their money, makes it the more important that strictly honest agencies should be multiplied for bringing together the employer and employed. At the same time the severely repressive enactments and high license fees which have been established in most states as a check to malpractices, have prevented us from advancing as rapidly as we could have desired.

Nevertheless in the last month for which our statistical particulars are available, we succeeded in finding work for no less than 4797 persons, being at the rate of nearly 60,000 per annum.

CHAPTER 17
KNIGHTS OF HOPE, FOR WORK AMONG PRISONERS

In many of the prisons throughout the country we are permitted to conduct regular services. In some of them we have been allowed to enroll the converts as Salvationists. The officials speak highly in regard to the good conduct of these men, and in times of emergency they have been known to render excellent service.

In one case a notorious murderer was converted, and was permitted to conduct a Bible-class among some eight men who were being tried or had been sentenced for a similar offense. This resulted in the conversion of several of the others.

But it has been the ex-criminal who has been the special object of our solicitude. When his sentence has expired his position is indeed painful. It is only natural that employers should be very unwilling to offer him work. But should he succeed in finding a place, he will commonly be blackmailed by his old associates and compelled to pay them nearly all his earnings, under threat of losing his position by his employer being informed about the past. In some cities it is the police themselves who embitter the life of the ex-criminal by a systematic persecution which often drives him to despair.

For hundreds of these men we have found temporary employment in our own establishments until we could safely recommend them to employers of labor, after satisfying ourselves of the genuineness of their reformation. In this way and with our guarantee they have been safe from the attacks of the blackmailer.

CHAPTER 18

WINTER RELIEF

The severe character of the winter in our northern states makes the provision of special winter relief a matter of urgent necessity.

" We prayed for the snow and eagerly watched the passing clouds," said one of the sufferers, now an officer in our ranks, " because then we knew there would be a chance of earning a dollar a day for sweeping it away."

It was stated not long ago that when 6000 shovels were given out by the city of New York for clearing the snow, there were 10 men fighting for each shovel. It seems hardly credible to think that 60,000 men, mostly with families dependent on them, should struggle fiercely for the privilege of standing in the bitter cold for 10 or 12 hours, with but little underclothing, and most of them without proper overcoats. And yet such was the case.

Regularly organized winter relief has been carried on by the Salvation army, and this on a vast scale. In the city of Detroit during a severe winter, when poverty and suffering were intense, our officers were used by the authorities and citi-

zens for the distribution of food and clothing to the value of
$200,000 an exact list being kept of the 7000 families assisted
and of the articles supplied.

During the severe blizzard of 1899, when traffic was par-
alyzed, and in many cases a coal famine prevailed, the doors
of our halls were thrown open throughout the country, and
those who could not obtain warmth and food in their tenements were cared for by thousands, the police and city authorities cooperating heartily with us in our efforts. Indeed
so terrible was the distress that the police stations and ar-
mories were officially thrown open in New York and instruc-
tions issued by the state and city authorities to supply food
and shelter to all who might appear to be in need. It was
then that one of the finest compliments was paid to the Salvation army by the poor of the city. Our halls and institutions were crowded to the doors, while but few availed themselves of the proffered hospitality of the state. Our large hall
and headquarters in 14th street accommodated nightly about
1000 persons, while from the regimental armory across the
street we received a polite request to supply coffee and bread
for 16 persons who had applied for help.

Fearing that the police stations might be as crowded as our
halls, and that it might be necessary to engage and fit up some
empty stores, we telephoned to the police headquarters to in-
quire what was the condition of affairs. " We have plenty of
room," was the reply. " All the people have gone to Booth
Tucker's show." We were, indeed, grateful to learn that in
their hour of need they should thus openly manifest their confidence and take advantage of the help we had provided.

CHAPTER 19

MEDICAL RELIEF

In a country which abounds with hospitals and medical relief, it may naturally be supposed that there has been but little
necessity for us to make any extensive additions to our respon-

sibilities in this direction. We have been glad to avail ourselves to the utmost of the generous assistance afforded us by existing institutions.

Nevertheless little by little work of this character has been forced upon us. The nursing of the sick in their own homes, the caring for maternity cases in the slums and in our rescue homes, the ministering to those of our own people who were ill, and the fact that we have now in our own ranks a considerable number of those who possess medical experience, have led to important expansions in this direction.

CHAPTER 20

SUMMER OUTINGS FOR THE POOR

To the children and women who have no opportunity of escaping from the scorching heat of our summers, the luxury of an occasional steamer-trip, or outing, can hardly be over-estimated. In Brooklyn, Philadelphia, Boston, Cleveland, Chicago and many other cities arrangements have been made for the careful distribution of tickets amongst those who need this form of relaxation the most. In many cases the street-car companies have cooperated with us by granting free transportation.

In Kansas City a summer camp has been established in one of the principal parks. Here tents are pitched and poor families have the privilege of spending a week at a time under the trees. Sick children at the point of death have been restored to life and health in an incredibly short space of time, to the joy of their parents.

CHAPTER 21

PENNY ICE WAGONS AND PENNY COLD DRINKS

Penny ice wagons and penny cold drinks have constituted another popular form of summer relief. In Kansas City our ice wagons pass regularly through the poor quarters, selling a large block of ice for a cent.

In Boston penny cold drinks have proved extremely popular and have helped to counteract the influences of the saloon.

CHAPTER 22

CHRISTMAS AND THANKSGIVING DINNERS

Our almost invariable rule is that whatever we do for a poor man must be paid for either in cash or labor. The price may be ridiculously low, or the task may be accomplished in an hour, and yet it must be something which he will feel is equivalent to the help which he receives. Thus we help without pauperizing.

At the same time we can not but feel that there are times when this rule should be relaxed and the poor should be invited to our table " without money and without price." The two annual occasions when this takes place are Thanksgiving day and Christmas day. On the former occasion we commonly provide for about 20,000 persons, while on last Christmas day we spread our table for 145,000. In New York alone 25,000 meals were provided, the vast and well-known Madison Square garden being engaged for the occasion. In Chicago, Boston, Cleveland, Philadelphia, St Louis and other large cities the number averaged from 5000 to 10,000.

Nor are the poor treated on these occasions as if they were paupers. Our officers and soldiers wait upon them personally, gladly sacrificing their own family enjoyments for the purpose, and treating them with loving heartiness. The tables are loaded generously with turkeys and cranberry sauce, with roast beef and pies, with fruit and crackers. Those who are prevented by illness and other domestic causes from attending in person, receive baskets filled with food in their garret-homes, and a link of love is forged between the needy, and the citizens of each city, the value of which in troublous times it is difficult to overestimate.

GROUP OF SLUM OFFICERS IN NEW YORK

CHAPTER 23

MISSING FRIENDS AND INQUIRY DEPARTMENT

Had America been discovered in his days, the prodigal son would surely have gone there! Certainly it is the favorite home of the modern prodigal.

At the time of writing we have no less than 1000 cases of inquiry under investigation. Quite recently an heir to an estate was hunted up by our officers, after the police had failed in their attempts to discover his whereabouts.

The fact that our *War cry* is published in 45 different countries and colonies, being translated into 26 languages, enables us to follow up clues from one country to another, our officers and soldiers gladly furnishing their services free of all expense in this mission of love.

CHAPTER 24

FARM COLONIES

THE LANDLESS MAN TO THE MANLESS LAND

Domicide, or the destruction of the family and the home, is one of the worst signs of modern civilization. "I have three brothers," said one of our Bowery boys, adding with the mother wit which often characterizes this class, "but only one is *living!* The other two are *married!*"

The pivot of true social reform turns upon the preservation or restoration of the *family unit*. Society must discover methods for dealing with its poor, which shall make it possible for them to marry and support their children in decency and comfort. Destroy the home and you destroy the nation. We must show the poor man how he can afford to get married.

The keenest anguish of a city life is that which centers round the starving family. The single man, or woman, is not to be so much pitied. It is much easier for such to pick up a living. Even if they fall, they fall alone.

It is far otherwise with the family. Here the finger-prints of poverty leave their blackest mark, and the suffering is the most appalling, because the victims consist so largely of weak women and innocent children and of the class who are eager to work if they have but the chance.

What has society to offer? The brand of pauperdom and the annihilation of the home! As a condition of its assistance, family ties must be severed. The father must go to this semi-penal institution, the mother to a second, and the children to a third. Even then, if the future presented some hope of re-union, the pauper's lot might be made more endurable. But no! "All hope abandon ye who enter here!" What wonder then that the poor hate a system which means the trampling upon the tenderest affections of the heart?

The very prosperity of our cities has attracted to many of them a larger population than they can absorb. For every thousand families who could obtain employment on a living wage, two and three thousand have flocked to our great man-ufacturing centers, with the inevitable result that our principal cities have been overcrowded with an increasing number of those who, if not absolutely dependent on public or private charity, eke out a hand-to-mouth existence of a painful and humiliating character.

How is this growing and ghastly evil to be combatted? Al-ready taxes have become so heavy in some places that it has been no uncommon thing for owners of property to abandon their rights through inability to bear the burden. The evil is visibly increasing year by year.

One class of reformers assert the absolute right of the " out-of-works " to be found employment by the state. But how is this to be done without seriously damaging the position of the " *in-works?* " The moment the produce of the labor of the " out-of-works " is thrown on to the market, it can hardly fail to lower the value of the goods they produce, and thereby lower the wages of the " in-works " with whom they compete,

A GROUP OF AMITY, COLO., COLONISTS.

OUR FIRST STABLE ON THE PRAIRIE.

and this on an unfair basis, inasmuch as they constitute cheap
and underpaid labor.

Now the farm colony plan avoids this difficulty altogether.
It says in brief: " Place the waste labor upon the waste land
by means of the waste capital, and thereby convert this trinity
of waste into a unity of production." It goes " one better "
than the mere " living wage " or " work for everybody " idea,
inasmuch as it proposes to recognize and maintain the family
unit, and to transform each workless family into a *home-maker*
and a *home-owner*, and this without imperilling the position of
the " in-works." On the contrary, the latter will be vastly bet-
tered, first by the removal of the terrible incubus of taxation,
and second by the fact that the multitudes thus happily removed
will immediately require the produce of the " in-works " labor,
thereby increasing the home demand enormously.

Suppose, for instance, as has been suggested by a leading
New York philanthropist, that a fund of $100,000,000
should be created for finding temporary employment for
the " out-of-works " in the cities where they at present
congregate. This would probably aggravate the evil instead
of mitigating it. For one thing it would enormously increase
the temptation, which is already drawing millions of our country population to the cities, by adding an element of apparent
security, since they would feel that if they failed to obtain
work for themselves, they could always fall back upon this fund.

Again, it would quickly be exhausted. Already $50,000,000
are being annually poured down the throats of our 3,000,000
submerged without producing any appreciable difference,
beyond prolonging their existence under circumstances, which
are alike degrading and dishonorable. As for really mitigating or removing the evil, it does not even pretend to do so,
and it may be fairly questioned whether our present system
does not daily and hourly aggravate it.

And yet the real remedy is so extremely simple that it seems
amazing that it has not been accepted and put into operation

long ago. The same money which is now absorbed year by
year, either in placing the " out-of-works " in cruel competition with the "in-works," or in training the former in habits
of idleness, while sacred family ties are ruthlessly shattered, and
vast and increasing hordes of homeless and hopeless men and
women created, to be a prey to the anarchist and a menace to
society — the same money, I venture to assert — only yearly
less of it, might be invested in buying land, erecting cottages,
and planting colonies of happy, home-owning families, who
would be a bulwark of strength to our nation.

On this plan, even that most hopeless and degraded production of our modern civilization, the genuine " *hobo*," would
be turned, if I may so play upon the word, into a " *homebo*,"
or at least a " *hopebo!* " Flash before the eyes of even our
criminal, as well as of our pauper, population, the possibility
of becoming, not merely the serfs of the soil or of the labor
employer, but *home-owners*, and it requires no prophet to discover that you will cut in two the present number of our institutions for these classes.

The existing annual expenditure of $50,000,000 would
suffice to remove from our cities 500,000 men, women and
children in families, at an average cost of $100 per head.
The money so laid out would be permanently and safely
invested, and would be secured by the " natural increment "
of the land thus densely peopled. The colonies would easily
pay 5% interest on the investment, and the entire outlay
would be repaid within, at the longest, from 10 to 15 years,
when it would be reinvested in planting another vast series
of colonies.

That this is no mere idle dream is proven by the experience
we have already gained on our three American colonies. In
Colorado, in California, and in Ohio, we have established ex-
perimental centers, the results of which have been eminently
satisfactory. We were told by many that so infatuated were

SALVATION ARMY WORKINGMEN'S INSTITUTE, SAN FRANCISCO CALIFORNIA

the poor with city life, that no persuasions would prevail on
them

a) to *go* to such colonies at all;

b) to *stay* on them if they did go;

c) to *work* with the industry which a farmer's life would
entail; and

d) to *pay* back the money expended in transplanting them.
It was also pointed out to us that the attempt to colonize had
often failed, even under the most favorable circumstances,
owing to the above causes.

But the failures of the past may always be traced to some
distinct cause, which should serve as a warning beacon to
future enterprise, and not for its discouragement. Because the
coast of the Atlantic is dotted with wrecks, shall we refuse to
found our New Yorks and Bostons? Nay, let us erect all the
needful lighthouses, mark with buoys the dangerous chan-
nels, blow up, if needs be, the Hell's Gate obstructions, and
then throw open our harbors to the commerce of the world!

Even so with our colonization plans, it will be found that
the failures of the past have been almost entirely due

a) to lack of proper organization;

b) to the spirit of self-seeking;

c) to the lack of capital; or

d) to the careless choice of unsuitable colonists.

All these causes are perfectly avoidable. They are rocks on
which common sense can build its warning signals, and of
which future enterprises can steer clear.

That America is singularly suited for operations of this
character, is proven by the fact that they are already being
carried on, quietly, but on a vast scale and with remarkable
success under our very eyes by the Mormons. From Idaho to
Arizona, from Nevada to Colorado, they are rapidly absorb-
ing under the homestead laws the richest and most fertile
valleys of the great Western plateau. Pastmasters in the art of
irrigation and cultivation, they are accumulating a wealth and

3

laying the foundations of a power, the extent of which it is difficult to overestimate.

Surely, it is high time that our vast Eastern centers of civilization and wealth from Chicago to New York, from Boston
to Washington, should wake up to the grand possibilities that
lie before them, and turn some of their immense accumulations
of non-interest-earning capital to the solution of the nation's
greatest problem, and its greatest need by the placing of the
landless man on the manless land.

This, I venture to prophesy, will be the coming battle-cry
of the philanthropist, the capitalist, and the statesman, while
to those interested in the spiritual and moral welfare of our
unchurched masses, it will seem all important that the leaven
of religion should be mingled with this dough of humanity in
its latter-day Exodus in search of a home Canaan!

That thousands in our crowded cities are eagerly waiting for
an opportunity to take part in that exodus, we can prove from
the list of some 5000 persons who have, without solicitation,
offered themselves to us for the purpose.

That they are willing to stay, to work, and to pay their
way, has also been abundantly proven by those whom we have
been able to send forth.

The Washington correspondent of the *Chicago record* recently visited our Colorado colony in company with the vice-
president of the Santa Fe R. R., Paul Morton, and its industrial
commissioner, James Davis. It was quite a " surprise visit,"
quite unexpected by either colonists or manager.

In a glowing two-column story, Mr Curtis gives the history of the enterprise. His concluding paragraphs contain the
following sentences:

There is no neater group of houses in Colorado, and no
more contented community in the world. Nearly everyone
has written to friends urging them to join the next colony that
comes out, and those I talked with were enthusiastic over their
success and the pleasures they enjoy. It was difficult for some
of them to find words to express their emotions. . . .

SALVATION ARMY SALVAGE WAREHOUSE, CHICAGO

The ranchmen and cowboys no longer make fun of the Salvation army colony. They recognize not only a great success, but a purpose also, and give the colonists their hea~v and cordial support.

The only serious difficulty that has been encountered by us, has been the lack of sufficient capital to conduct the enterprise on a broad and national basis. With an outlay of $60,000 we have been enabled on our three colonies to erect about 60 cottages, locate about 200 men, women and children as colonists, pay traveling, freight, and installments on land, purchase about 100 horses and 200 cows, as well as pigs and poultry, together with machinery and general outfit, besides meeting the living expenses of our colonists for nearly two years. The outlay is in every case more than covered by the greatly enhanced value of the land thus thickly settled, each colonist having from five to twenty acres allotted to him, the exact amount varying according to the quality of the soil, the value of the land and the nearness of the market. On our Colorado colony we cleared more than $1000 last year (1899) by the sale of our canteloupe crop alone, and our creamery is already bringing the colonists a cash income of $3000 per year. Of the 14 families who formed the original settlers, 18 months ago, and of the 12 additional families who have since joined them, all but one are self-supporting, and the solitary exception is due to illness. Strangely enough he is the only single colonist, the others being married, and mostly with large families.

The following prominent citizens have warmly advocated this system of dealing with the poor, and have cordially cooperated with us in our work: The late Governor Roswell P. Flower, of New York; ex-Governor Alva Adams, of Colorado; Governor Hazen Pingree, of Michigan; Hon. Benjamin F. Tracy, former secretary to the navy; Hon. Charles F. MacLean, justice of the supreme court of New York; Hon. John E. Milholland, former editor of the *Tribune*, New York; Hon.

Josiah Quincy, former mayor of Boston; Hon. Platt Rogers, former mayor of Denver; Hon. James D. Phelan, mayor of San Francisco; Hon. L. R. Ellert, former mayor of San Francisco; Hon. Luther Laflin Mills, attorney, Chicago; Hon. Myron T. Herrick, president Bank of savings, Cleveland; Rabbi Voorsanger, of San Francisco; E. P. Ripley, Esq., president of the Santa Fe R. R.; John E. Searles, esq., of New York; Claus Spreckles, esq., of San Francisco; Daniel Meyer, esq., of San Francisco.

At the Sixth national irrigation congress, the following resolution was unanimously passed:

Resolved, That we have heard with great interest and great pleasure Mrs Booth Tucker's presentation and explanation of the purposes of the Salvation army in organizing colonies of the worthy poor in our great cities to settle and build homes on the rich irrigated lands of the west. This is a grand, noble and patriotic work, and deserves the earnest commendation and support of every citizen of our country. The west extends a hearty welcome to these people, and we pledge our sympathy and support in aiding these people to make happy homes upon our rich and productive land.— *Lincoln, Nebraska*, September, 1897

The fact that we have so large a number of social relief establishments, accommodating about 7000 persons, scattered throughout the principal cities of the United States, and that in addition to this our 704 corps and slum posts bring us into constant and immediate contact with the masses of the needy poor, who have the utmost confidence in our good faith, and know that we are not trying to exploit them in the interests of some land boom or speculative scheme, places us in a specially favorable position for handling such an enterprise. We are able, without any additional expense, to carefully sift and train our colonists before sending them out, and to re-absorb in city life those of them who may not prove to be adapted to the colony.

At the same time, our military and methodical system of

SALVATION ARMY JUNK SHOP, CHICAGO

management enables us to handle these colonists, and to organize and weld them into one harmonious whole in a manner
which would otherwise be very difficult.

Certainly it may be said, without hesitation, that there are
few branches of sociology, which possess more interest for the
student of pauperology. Our farm colonies differ from ordinary
poor farms in the same way that our ordinary city institutions
differ from a prison. There is nothing of a penal character
about them. The colonist is not a mere day-laborer without
any direct interest in the soil. He is not separated from his
family. The links of love are strengthened, instead of being
relaxed, and he has placed before him the bright possibility of
becoming a home-owner, while the element of doubt and fear
in regard to the future of his children, is removed by the fact
that they, too, can marry, settle down and become home-
owners like himself, of a similar cottage and lot, without the
necessity of being dependent on his earnings or on what he
may leave them when he dies. The son and daughter have as
good a chance of a start in life as their parents, without any
of the bitter experiences through which the latter have passed.
At the same time there is nothing to prevent the brightest
members of the family from entering legal, mercantile or other
professions.

In view of the existing plethora of educational and medical
philanthropies, is it too much to hope that America will lead
the way along this new line of sociology, and prove to the
nations of the world that a poor man properly handled can be
a greater source of national wealth than any gold mine which
has yet been discovered.

The Salvation Army as a Temperance Movement

CHAUTAUQUA
ADDRESS

By Commander Booth Tucker

THE SALVATION ARMY
AS A TEMPERANCE
MOVEMENT

Being Notes of an Address at the
Chautauqua Assembly,
New York

BY

COMMANDER BOOTH TUCKER

The Reliance Trading Company
Printers and Bookbinders
New York City

THE SALVATION ARMY AS A TEMPERANCE MOVEMENT

FOR thirty-eight years The Salvation Army has waged a ceaseless war against drink. And yet, during the twenty-two years that I have been an officer in its ranks, I cannot remember once giving, or hearing one of our officers give, a temperance lecture. When, therefore, your press bureau asked me for a summary of my address, I was obliged to confess that I had not even an outline to fall back on. To approach this august and world-famous assembly with my "maiden" effort on this line seems such pre-

3

sumption on my part that I have been repenting of it ever since I accepted the cordial invitation extended to me by your President. Those of you who are including Sanscrit—that Italian of the Orient—in your course of study will understand me when I give vent to my feelings in the words of the famous Hindoo poet Kalidasa:

"Titîrshur dushtaram mohâd udupen-âsmi sâgaram."

("In my folly I am like some tiny skiff which seeks to cross the stormy ocean.")

And yet I think I may say that the work of The Salvation Army is in itself a temperance lecture of the most fascinating and practical character. I trust that in confining my remarks to it here this afternoon I shall not be thought to be in any sense ignoring or depreciating the noble work put in by so many other organizations. I am only obeying your President's orders in keeping to my subject. I have the highest regard for the W. C. T. U., and other kindred organizations.

1. Every Salvationist whom you meet, every worker in our ranks, every officer, every bandsman, every member is a teetotaller. Abstinence is a condition of membership.

2. We do not simply write, and speak, and legislate against drink. We pursue it to its darkest haunts. The slum, the tenement, the saloon, the dive, the brothel are boldly attacked and regularly visited by our officers. This is no spasmodic crusade. At every one of our 7,000 centres throughout the world, our 15,000 officers and employees, our 45,000 local officers, or deacons, our

5

16,000 brass bandsmen, our 50,000 musicians and hundreds of thousands of active workers are carrying on a daily campaign, in which at least 500,000 meetings are held monthly, attended each month by at least 50,000,000 persons, in 45 different countries and colonies, using 31 different languages.

What is the result of these meetings? That is a fair question. We could not be happy without definite results. We regard these as the evidence of the wisdom or unsuitablity of our plans. We judge ourselves by them. We desire others to judge us in the same way. They are carefully tabulated for our guidance week by week. Thus I can give you the exact history of every corps in this country from its start.

The keynote of our temperance

work is conversion, and our records show that during the past ten years from 200,000 to 250,000 persons have yearly professed conversion throughout the world, making a total for the decade of more than 2,000,000. To God alone we give the glory! Here in the United States the number has averaged from 35,000 to 50,000 each year, a glorious total of some 400,000 conversions in the brief space of ten years.

We may fairly estimate that not less than ten per cent. of these have been converted drunkards—200,000 in the world, 40,000 in this country, in ten years. Do they stand? Not all, by any means. Some of them require a lot of spiritual pick-me-ups and tonics. Yet we have to-day in our world-wide ranks at least 100,000 who have been saved from lives of drunkenness, while tens of thousands more have been added to the churches. Our treasurer at Canandaigua, N. Y., is a lady who, with her husband, could recollect having had more than 200 convictions. We have in our ranks at Buffalo 15 drunkards who served 52 years between them, and cost the State $49,600.

The assistant pastors of two leading churches in one of our great cities were saved from drink through the direct work of The Army. One of them had, previous to his conversion, dragged his wife by her hair out of their home and thrown her into the canal in a fit of drunken fury. The pastor whom he assists is to-day one of the best-known men in the country.

In all cases we aim at the definite

conversion of the drunkard, and herein lies one great secret of our success.

If I am asked to what further facts or measures do we attribute our success, I would reply, that it is because we have discovered and dealt with the *causes* of the dreaded evil. We have *located the Bacillus Drink-oxera*. We have studied his habits. We have found out the various tribes, or species, into which he may be divided, the miasmic breeding grounds which give him birth, and the remedies which may best be applied for his extinction.

When epidemics of cholera, of yellow fever, or of typhoid, ravage a city, the doctors are at once busy dealing with the cause. Is it the sewerage that is the source of trouble? It must be purified, flushed,

9

and, if necessary, reconstructed, no matter what the cost. Is it the water, or milk, or fruit, or fish, or meat, or the use of acids in canned goods, that constitute the source of infection? No measures are too radical, no sacrifice too great, to combat and overcome the evil. *Remedy the cause and you will remedy the disease,* is the great principle on which all reformatory action is based.

Society's moral sewerage needs similar purification. It has been too long neglected. We have dealt *too much* with the *manifestation* and *too little* with the *cause.* Those sewers which radiate through our great centres of population are infected with other bacilli besides the drinkoxera —bacilli which help to give to the latter its vitality and deadliness. They are intimately related to each

10

other. It is often difficult to ascertain or draw the exact line where one commences and the other leaves off. All we can say is, that to effectively eradicate the one you must recognize and deal with the other. Whether occupying the position of cause or of effect, they must be unitedly studied and unitedly remedied, if the cure is to be permanent and effective.

There is the *Wantoxera Bacillus*—the world's sewerage of want. How deadly is the miasma, how noxious are the vapors that proceed from these lethal swamps!

It is well that we should familiarize ourselves with their extent and character, or at least with some of their worst phases. Eight hundred thousand immigrants landed on our shores during the last twelve months. It is expected that upwards of

11

one million more will arrive during the ensuing year. What preparations have been made for their reception, for housing, and providing them with work? None whatever. We leave to Pro idence what we should deal with ourselves.

What becomes of them? They are sandwiched in among our already overcrowded slum and tenement population. Let Mr. Jacob Riis, the well-known expert on this question, speak. He tells us in his recent volume, "The Battle with the Slums," how in one tenement which was supposed to accommodate sixteen families, providing three rooms for each, he found forty-seven families, each limited to a single room. When the visit of the inspector was to be avoided the door would be kept fastened for a time till the extra families

12

had taken their departure via the fire escape, only to return after the inspector had gone.

In one case he found a family of six, the parents nd four children, occupying one bed, four in it, and the other two laid crosswise at the foot of the bed.

In London a recent census shows that conditions are still worse. Here it was found that 3,000 families, consisting of nine souls, occupied one room, while 7,000 families of eight. and 23,000 numbering six or seven, were similarly situated. The ordinary furniture of each room was one bed. Those who could slept in it, and the others under it, because it was the warmest place in the room and they could not afford a fire. In one case that was brought to our notice, a family actually drew a chalk line across the floor and rented half its room to a second family, while the latter shortly afterwards took in a "boarder" to further reduce its rent!

In Berlin official statistics were carefully prepared which revealed the fact that the mortality in these one-roomed homes averaged 163 per 1,000!

Can you wonder, then, that amid environments so wretched, so infinitely miserable, so unworthy of our Christianity, philanthropy and education, drinkshops should reap a rich harvest of results, or that a man will spend his last cent to exchange such heathenish surroundings for the brightness and gaiety of a saloon or the momentary oblivion of a drunken bout? Is it not safe to assume that to permanently destroy the drink habit we must go further, and remedy this blatant cause? In

Did time permit I could take you through other regions of a similar character. Seven thousand of our working girls in Ohio were found to be earning, on an average, $4.80 per week—many less. The merchants of a certain western city would take typewriters from the business colleges on trial for two or three months without salary, and then discharge them as unsuitable. They were *mighty hard to please!*

Again you have the *Doloxera Bacillus,* which flourishes in the world's sewerage of woe. Take but one department of this wilderness of misery. It is estimated that there are some 300,000 fallen women in this country. They are, almost without exception, the victims of drink.

They could not ply their miserable vocation without its help. Their lives are said to average but five years. This means that some 60,000 of them yearly pass to a nameless and dishonored grave, while from the ranks of virtue, of our youth, beauty and womanhood, the gaps are more than made good by a yearly holocaust of 60,000 souls.

During the last eight years we have established throughout the world some 120 Homes for the Fallen, and through these about 5,000 girls pass annually. Some 40,000 have already, to our knowledge, been restored to lives of virtue, saved from a drunkard's and a harlot's grave. Here in America we have 21 Homes, accommodating 500 girls, and through these Homes some 2,000 passed during the last twelve

months, our records showing that
91 per cent. of these have been permanently reclaimed from lives of
drunkenness and vice.

And yet there are those who think
that reclamation in such cases is
well-nigh impossible. One of our
Homes was visited by a judge who
had been for some time a subscriber.
He was pleased with its appearance
and management, but confessed to
the assistant officer who was showing him around that he did not believe in the permanent restoration
of any girl who had once embarked
on such a life. "Could you tell me,"
he said, "of a single instance where
a genuine and lasting change took
place?"

"Why, certainly I can," said the
officer. "We have a girl in this
Home who is the daughter of well-

to-do parents. She was carefully
brought up, received a good education, and was finally engaged to a
young man who cruelly deceived her
and then deserted her. She left her
home to hide her shame, and then
she took to drink to forget her sorrow, till she became a habitual and
hopeless drunkard. The magistrates
and police were tired of dealing with
her. One day, as the laundry wagon
of our Home was passing down the
road, she was seen lying helplessly
drunk near the sidewalk, with some
boys making fun of her. Our officers
picked her up, strapped her on to the
wagon, brought her home and put
her to bed. It was some days before
any impression could be made upon
her, but at length she broke completely down, was blessedly converted, and has now been a useful

13

worker for the past three years."

"Can I see her?" said the judge, who had been greatly impressed by the grace, tact and modesty of the speaker.

"Why, certainly," was the reply. "You are speaking to her at this moment." The judge was dumb-founded. Tears sprang to his eyes, and he became thenceforth a staunch champion of the work.

Why, it may be asked, is there so much vice? One great reason is the increasing notion abroad among the working classes that they cannot afford to get married. Seven hundred and thirty-nine out of 1,000 marriageable persons in London are unmarried, 261 married. It should be our great aim to make it possible for the workingman to have his home and family.

And then there is the *Crimoxera Bacillus,* which haunts the world's sewerage of wickedness and crime. Our prison population in America numbers 84,000, while there are probably not less than half a million criminals outside. It is safe to calculate that not less than ninety per cent. drink hard and often. They are compelled to do so by their associations and surroundings. The burglar's plans are laid in a saloon, his spoils are shared there, and it is there that the detective knows where to find his man. And yet to prove that a large percentage of our criminal population is reclaimable would not be difficult. The Deputy Commissioner of Corrections in New York told me recently that in his opinion seventy-five per cent. of our burglars would quit their evil ways if they had a fair and square chance for making an honest livelihood. But who wants to employ an ex-burglar?

Now it is amongst these moral sewers of want, woe and wickedness that you will find the saloon flourishes. It cannot make a living in the "silk stocking" districts and Chautauquas! It would die of inanition.

I say, therefore, once more, that to deal successfully with drink you must *remedy the cause!* We believe that we have discovered some valuable *antitoxines* which are well suited for this purpose. I may classify them under four heads, for the sake of fixing them in your minds, and if in doing so I venture to take some further liberties with English as it is spoken in Chautauqua. I think I may claim that your

21

own name has afforded me a dangerous and tempting precedent, and I
trust I shall not unduly shock our
honored Principal and Chairman in
so doing.

There are four distinct species of
remedies which we advocate, and
which, from experience, we are able
to say have rendered us excellent
service in the case of the terrible
maladies which I have sought to
describe.

(a) *Laboroxine,* or, *Work for all.*

(b) *Domoxine,* or, *Homes for all.*

(c) *Bread - and - Butteroxine,* or,
Food for all, and

(d) *Salvoxine,* or *Salvation for
all.*

You ask, *Can it be done?* I reply,
It is being done and this already on
a vast scale which has surprised
statesmen, philanthropists and ré-

22

ligious leaders. Our Social Relief
Institutions in America now provide
a nightly pillow for some 8,500 men,
1,000 women and 650 children. During the last year we found some
three million beds for the needy
classes, besides cheap coal, fuel,
clothing and furniture, with free
Thanksgiving and Christmas dinners. The total outlay amounted to
about $800,000, of which all but
about $50,000 was raised by the work
or payments of the people helped.

Our Industrial Homes and Labor
Bureaux find shelter, food and work
for the unemployed. These Homes
use the waste labor of a city in collecting the waste material, in putting it into marketable shape, and in
obtaining from its sale the wherewithal to carry on the work. If a
man comes to us a physical and

moral wreck, in rags and tatters, without a cent in his possession and with the marks of sin only too plainly stamped upon his face, what do we do? We do not harden our hearts against him. He is a human being, with the stamp of God's creative Hand still upon him—the dim reflection of His glory still lingers in those marred and drink-soaked lineaments. On the other hand we do not pauperize him. We take him to our Industrial Home. Here he is bathed and cleansed and shaved. His ragged, vermin-stricken garments are exchanged for decent second-hand clothing, collected by our wagons. He is fed—perhaps he has not had a square meal for weeks. It is so easy to get a drink for nothing, when neither food, work nor money can be obtained by a man whose very

24

appearance stamps him as a tramp or "hobo." What if he be a hobo? Let us see if we cannot make him, first, a "hopebo," and, ultimately, a "homebo!" One such was found swinging to a tree in a rich quarter of New York. His clothing consisted of a ragged coat and pants, with shoes that were held together by pieces of string. He had not a cent in his possession. In his pocket was a scrap of paper on which his last message to society was written in a hand of which no Chautauquan need have been ashamed:

"They say I am a hobo! I guess that's right! A woman told me to-day I ought to kill myself. I guess that's right! Well, here goes! Good luck to you! Maybe you had a better chance than poor old

JOE."

He was but one of many, despaired of by society, till he came to despair of himself and ended his miserable career. But, thank God, thousands upon thousands of those just as ragged and wretched and hopeless as he are being reached, rescued and reformed by our Industrial Homes! Our threefold recipe of *"Soup, Soap and Salvation"* has been successfully applied. Over some of these Homes have been inscribed the words, *"No one need steal, starve or commit suicide,"* while over the gates of all might be written, *"Despair abandon, ye who enter here!"* Our Laboroxine serum has worked wonders, and we have found that ninety-five per cent. of the unemployed are willing to work if they are given a fair chance.

Still more successful has been our

Domoxine remedy of Homes for all.
I do not here refer so much to our
Workingmen's and Workingwomen's
Hotels, or Homes for Women and
Children, as to our Farm Colonies,
where the worthy but poor family
has an opportunity of becoming a
home owner. On all our three
colonies total abstinence is enforced,
being a condition of membership.
Here we take the deserving family
and provide it with cottage, farm,
live stock and implements. Some
five years ago I said, "Place this
waste labor upon the waste land by
means of waste capital, and thereby
convert this trinity of waste into a
unity of production." In other
words, place the landless man upon
the manless land. It was prophesied
that they would neither go, nor stay,
neither work, nor pay! But we are

27

able to-day to point to the fact that hundreds have gone and stayed, have worked and paid, while thousands more are eagerly waiting to follow.

On one of these colonies last year the settlers averaged a cash income of $850 per family, besides having abundance of food for their families and live stock. On another they formed a Commercial Club, which included some twenty businesses and had a turnover last year of about $200,000, paying to the railroad about $50,000 for freight. Stone cottages and barns dot the 2,000 acres of rich irrigated land where this colony is situated, and the twenty-acre farms, with their improvements, are worth to-day from $2,000 to $5,000 each, while the families are self-supporting and prosperous. No liquor is sold, and the only drunkards who are seen are those who travel many miles from the surrounding country to attend our meetings, with the result that many of these also have been converted, and some have settled on our lands.

When our first party of pioneers arrived at this colony five years ago they were given temporary shelter in a shed, which was known as the "Opera House," of a near-by village. The night before their arrival there had been a dance which was attended by the cowboys for miles abroad. One of their number fiddled, while the rest danced. "Jim," said one of the cowboys to the fiddler, "play so and so." "Sorry, but I don't know it," was the response. "I tell you, play so and so," repeated the cowboy, drawing his sixshooter. Then followed a fight, in which pistols were fired, the bullet marks from which adorned the walls when our pioneers took possession the following night. The fiddler is now one of our colonists. He has married and settled and has a happy home, while the cow punchers and bronco busters love to attend our meetings and listen to the music of our brass and string bands. Some of them are still a little unruly at times, but the oldest inhabitant of the place testifies enthusiastically to the wonderful change that has been wrought. The daring holdups and robberies that used to be planned have been exchanged for songs of salvation, and her own son is married to the eldest daughter of one of our most successful colonists and occupies a snug cottage on the town site.

As the elevated train was pulling out of a depot in New York a few weeks since, a child who was standing by its mother's side lost its balance and fell through the open window. It caught the railing and hung for a moment over the heads of the horrified crowd. Some workmen rushed to the spot, and as the child fell they caught it in their arms. Wonderful to relate, it was unhurt. Then placing it on the shoulder of the tallest workman, the crowd moved in a mass to the next depot. On its arrival there the entire train-load of passengers, filled with sympathy for the agonized and weeping mother, left the cars and were rushing to the spot where the accident had taken place, and where they expected to find the mangled corpse of the child. Midway the two crowds met. Overcome with joy at the sight of her child, safe and unhurt, the mother fainted away.

Hanging from the elevated railroads of our modern civilization may be seen to-day not one but tens of thousands of men, women and children. Beneath them yawns a terrible abyss. Drink, want, woe and wickedness are pushing them over the edge before our very eyes. With outspread arms The Salvation Army stands with its various agencies, seeking to remedy the causes of this wilderness of human woe, and bringing the sufferers in touch with the Calvary-provided remedy. We seek, we claim your sympathy and prayers.

Religion in America
Series II

An Arno Press Collection

Adler, Felix. **Creed and Deed:** A Series of Discourses. New York, 1877.

Alexander, Archibald. **Evidences of the Authenticity, Inspiration, and Canonical Authority of the Holy Scriptures.** Philadelphia, 1836.

Allen, Joseph Henry. **Our Liberal Movement in Theology:** Chiefly as Shown in Recollections of the History of Unitarianism in New England. 3rd edition. Boston, 1892.

American Temperance Society. **Permanent Temperance Documents of the American Temperance Society.** Boston, 1835.

American Tract Society. **The American Tract Society Documents, 1824-1925.** New York, 1972.

Bacon, Leonard. **The Genesis of the New England Churches.** New York, 1874.

Bartlett, S[amuel] C. **Historical Sketches of the Missions of the American Board.** New York, 1972.

Beecher, Lyman. **Lyman Beecher and the Reform of Society:** Four Sermons, 1804-1828. New York, 1972.

[Bishop, Isabella Lucy Bird.] **The Aspects of Religion in the United States of America.** London, 1859.

Bowden, James. **The History of the Society of Friends in America.** London, 1850, 1854. Two volumes in one.

Briggs, Charles Augustus. **Inaugural Address and Defense,** 1891-1893. New York, 1972.

Colwell, Stephen. **The Position of Christianity in the United States,** in Its Relations with Our Political Institutions, and Specially with Reference to Religious Instruction in the Public Schools. Philadelphia, 1854.

Dalcho, Frederick. **An Historical Account of the Protestant Episcopal Church, in South-Carolina,** from the First Settlement of the Province, to the War of the Revolution. Charleston, 1820.

Elliott, Walter. **The Life of Father Hecker.** New York, 1891.

Gibbons, James Cardinal. **A Retrospect of Fifty Years.** Baltimore, 1916. Two volumes in one.

Hammond, L[ily] H[ardy]. **Race and the South:** Two Studies, 1914-1922. New York, 1972.

Hayden, A[mos] S. **Early History of the Disciples in the Western Reserve, Ohio;** With Biographical Sketches of the Principal Agents in their Religious Movement. Cincinnati, 1875.

Hinke, William J., editor. **Life and Letters of the Rev. John Philip Boehm:** Founder of the Reformed Church in Pennsylvania, 1683-1749. Philadelphia, 1916.

Hopkins, Samuel. **A Treatise on the Millennium.** Boston, 1793.

Kallen, Horace M. **Judaism at Bay:** Essays Toward the Adjustment of Judaism to Modernity. New York, 1932.

Kreider, Harry Julius. **Lutheranism in Colonial New York.** New York, 1942.

Loughborough, J. N. **The Great Second Advent Movement:** Its Rise and Progress. Washington, 1905.

M'Clure, David and Elijah Parish. **Memoirs of the Rev. Eleazar Wheelock, D.D.** Newburyport, 1811.

McKinney, Richard I. **Religion in Higher Education Among Negroes.** New Haven, 1945.

Mayhew, Jonathan. **Observations on the Charter and Conduct of the Society for the Propagation of the Gospel in Foreign Parts;** Designed to Shew Their Non-conformity to Each Other. Boston, 1763.

Mott, John R. **The Evangelization of the World in this Generation.** New York, 1900.

Payne, Bishop Daniel A. **Sermons and Addresses, 1853-1891.** New York, 1972.

Phillips, C[harles] H. **The History of the Colored Methodist Episcopal Church in America: Comprising Its Organization, Subsequent Development, and Present Status.** Jackson, Tenn., 1898.

Reverend Elhanan Winchester: Biography and Letters. New York, 1972.

Riggs, Stephen R. **Tah-Koo Wah-Kan; Or, the Gospel Among the Dakotas.** Boston, 1869.

Rogers, Elder John. **The Biography of Eld. Barton Warren Stone, Written by Himself: With Additions and Reflections.** Cincinnati, 1847.

Booth-Tucker, Frederick. **The Salvation Army in America: Selected Reports, 1899-1903.** New York, 1972.

Satolli, Francis Archbishop. **Loyalty to Church and State.** Baltimore, 1895.

Schaff, Philip. **Church and State in the United States** or the American Idea of Religious Liberty and its Practical Effects with Official Documents. New York and London, 1888. (Reprinted from *Papers of the American Historical Association, Vol. II, No. 4.*)

Smith, Horace Wemyss. **Life and Correspondence of the Rev. William Smith, D.D.** Philadelphia, 1879, 1880. Two volumes in one.

Spalding, M[artin] J. **Sketches of the Early Catholic Missions of Kentucky: From Their Commencement in 1787 to the Jubilee of 1826-7.** Louisville, 1844.

Steiner, Bernard C., editor. **Rev. Thomas Bray: His Life and Selected** Works Relating to Maryland. Baltimore, 1901. (Reprinted from *Maryland Historical Society Fund Publication, No. 37.*)

To Win the West: Missionary Viewpoints, 1814-1815. New York, 1972.

Wayland, Francis and H. L. Wayland. **A Memoir of the Life and Labors of Francis Wayland, D.D., LL.D.** New York, 1867. Two volumes in one.

Willard, Frances E. **Woman and Temperance: Or, the Work and Workers** of the Woman's Christian Temperance Union. Hartford, 1883.